# It's All for the GOOD?

10 SOLUTIONS FOR A SEARCHING SOUL

# It's All for the GO⬤⬤D?

## A Simple Yet Deep Approach to Gaining Clarity on Your Life's Purpose

Rav Nachum Chaimowitz

ISBN: 978-965-572-165-2

Second printing: 5777/ 2017

Lev Yisrael, Inc.
POB 816
Monsey, N.Y. 11952
levyisrael@gmail.com

Distributed by:
Judaica Distribution Center Inc.
501 Prospect Street
Lakewood NJ 08701
www.israelbookshoppublications.com

Design: Ben Gasner Studio, Jerusalem

# RABBI SHMUEL KAMENETSKY

[Translated from the Hebrew]

*B'Siyata D'Shmaya, Elul, 5776*

The Mesilas Yeshorim has written in Chapter One and these are his words: "The foundation of devoutness and the source of the genuine service is, that it be clarified and true to a person what his obligation is in his world and toward what he needs to place his focus and aspiration in all that he works [for] all the days of his life."

"And behold, what *Chazal* have taught us is that man was created only to take pleasure upon Hashem and to enjoy from the shine of His *Shechinah* (G-dly Presence), which is really the true delight and the greatest pleasures of all the pleasures that can possibly exist".

Just like in regard to each and every *mitzvah*, it is not possible to fulfill appropriately unless one learns and also delves into it thoroughly to study its rules, its details and all its fine distinctions; most certainly it is so in regard to the topic of "a person's obligation is in his world" – "in all that he works [for] all the days of his life", that it is not possible to fulfill appropriately unless one learns and also delves into it thoroughly to understand its details and its fine distinctions.

Behold, Rav Nachum Chaimowitz *shlita* has come before me, and in his hand a manuscript that he compiled in the language which is spoken [in this country], clarifying foundations of *Jewish-life outlook* and their sources with respect to what the Ramchal *z"l* has written: "that man was created only to take pleasure upon Hashem". Although in the time of the Ramchal this sentence itself was enough to arouse the people of his generation to know what "a person's obligation in his world" [was], nowadays, in our generation, there has become a greater need for additional detail and clarification of this topic. And [this applies] especially to those who live in the diaspora and are not familiar in the language of the books that speak about this.

And behold I give a blessing to Rav Nachum *shlita* that he be successful in the work of his hands and that he merit to be counted among those who bring merit to the many. And in the merit of this study he should merit to strengthen members of our generation with a keen understanding of this important topic, and may he plant in their hearts [the desire] to fulfill "their obligation in their world" and to be aroused to the service of Hashem that [should] become true [and clarified] to them.

# RABBI MOSHE WOLFSON

## [Translated from the Hebrew]

*B'Siyata D'Shmaya, Month of Menachem Av, 5775*

Behold it was brought before me '[blessed] pages' from Rav Nachum Chaimowitz *shlita* – whom I am acquainted with now for numerous years – who merited to perform great and fortified deeds among the English-speaking *Ba'al Tshuvah* community as *Rosh Yeshiva* of the Lev Yisrael Yeshiva in Bet Shemesh. In the context of that position he dealt for many years in delivering the foundations of the *Jewish-life outlook* to returning souls in a language that is clear and comprehensible even for beginners, together with a clarification of [the] sources. And now he has come before me with a compilation of these foundations in an orderly fashion and in the spoken language [of the country].

And I saw his writings and summaries and they are truly explanations that can be understood by everyone. In my understanding this can be of great benefit to clarify and to review these foundations, especially nowadays – because there are many who have questions on these topics and they do not know the source answers to their questions, which were really already explained and dealt with and clarified in the holy writings.

Behold I bless the author that his *sefer* be received with an uplifted sense of appeal, and that through it may be strengthened many weak and rejected hearts in these generations. And may the author merit to compile additional important *seforim* [and merit] healthiness of body and an expanded sense of knowledge, and may we all merit to the coming of Mashiach our righteous (leader), soon in actuality, speedily in our days, Amen.

בברכת התורה

משה וואלפסאן

# CONTENTS

*Disclaimer:*

The concepts presented in this book do not represent original ideas of the author but are rather meant to elucidate ideas that are already found in classic Torah sources.

There is no intent whatsoever by the author to alter or to change the intention of any of the original sources.

The main sources are quoted in their original Hebrew form as an appendix to this publication.

# CONTENTS AT A GLANCE

*It's All for the Good* is organized with headings in such a way that can support quick-reference when needed. The headings will help you to skip around and easily find the source for any of the foundational axioms you are seeking to clarify.

*Here is a list of chapter summaries to know what's where:*

## AUTHOR'S PREFACE
## Why This Book Was Written

The Author's Preface tells you a little about the author and why he unequivocally decided to apply himself to this undertaking.

## PREFACE
## How to Use This Book

Here you can find tips as to how you can derive maximum benefit from this book. It also directs you where to read if you only have limited time.

## INTRODUCTION
## Why is it so Necessary Today to Impart the Message of a Jewish Soul's Purpose?

The introduction stands as an essay on its own. It explains the reason as to why *hashkafah* (Jewish life-outlook) was not a greatly emphasized Torah topic in previous generations – the experience of the Jewish lifestyle was *tangible* to all. Precisely for that reason – that the experience of the Jewish lifestyle is *not* so tangible nowadays – it needs to be greatly emphasized as a Torah topic in our times today.

## CHAPTER 1
## It All Starts with Your Axioms

In this first chapter you'll find the "stage being set" for verifying the purpose of life. You will begin to realize the importance of "axioms" in every discussion – and especially *the first axiom* from where everything begins. Also find out that it is a necessity to have *the same* axioms before beginning any debate – if you ever hope to come to any true and agreeable consensus with your opponent.

## CHAPTER 2
## The First Basic Axiom: Who Is Hashem?

Here's the real starting point for all of the axioms that follow. Everything we live for is built upon the premise of *"Adon Olam"* (there is a Creator of the world). But how do we understand who the Creator Really Is? This chapter will give you insight and explanation about who you have been referring to throughout your life whenever you mentioned the name: "Hashem".

## CHAPTER 3
## What Everyone in the World is *Really* Looking For

Read this fascinating chapter if you want to have a clearer idea as to *why* most people in the world choose something as their life's goal and purpose over another. What is it that makes a person choose something specific to 'dedicate his life to'? Is there really any one goal or purpose which is objectively 'better' than all the others?

## CHAPTER 4
## How Can I Know for Sure that Hashem is Here?

Discover a tool that can give you the certainty of inner conviction that you were always looking for. You grew up learning that Hashem is listening to you — but how can you know for sure? Start to apply the rules which emanate clearly from the words of our Sages and begin to recognize *for yourself* that Hashem's Presence is "Alive and Well" among us today just as it was in previous generations.

## CHAPTER 5
## What's Hashem's Goal?

Here's an answer to the classic question: "So if Hashem is Infinite and He doesn't need anything outside of Himself, why did He create us in the first place? What was *His* Intent in creation?" Reading this Chapter is also bound to cause a paradigm shift in the preconceived notions of all those who are occupied with configuring the amounts of punishment and Gehinom that Hashem may give them if they don't live up to their obligations.

# CHAPTER 6
## Why This World?

Once you are clear regarding Hashem's Intent for all of creation, the next question that arises is: "So why can't He just accomplish that goal in the most comfortable and convenient way possible? Why does He have to do it in such a way that we need to come *to this world* – which is clearly not such an good place?" This Chapter also includes a description of the greater "*task*" that Hashem has sent our souls down to this world for.

# CHAPTER 7
## How Can A Human Being "Become One" with Hashem?

This chapter clarifies the specific way that we work toward our goal of "becoming one" with Hashem. What exactly does that mean? Certainly a human being cannot "become Hashem". Learn about the different levels of how we grow throughout life in becoming "closer and closer" to Hashem by *building a relationship*.

# CHAPTER 8
## Feeling Hashem's Tangible Reality through Experience

Learn this amazing chapter to find out about one of the major tools available to us in building our relationship with Hashem. Since we believe that Hashem is Infinite, how is it possible for us to have any interaction with Him in a way that we can grasp *anything* 'about Him' at all? When used properly, this magnificent tool of "*experience*" can lead us over time to levels of overflowing positive emotions for Hashem.

# CHAPTER 9
## Can't Hashem Just "Help Us Out"?

Why is it that Hashem assumes a more 'passive role' when it comes to accomplishing things in this world? Find out the foundational answer to "If the Jewish nation is really His chosen people, why doesn't Hashem just intervene on their behalf and take them out of their exile already — both on the personal and the collective levels?" Also, check at the beginning of this chapter if you are looking for a 'power-point' review of all the axioms together. The last axiom on the 'list of axioms' for the "ultimate goal of our lives" is at the end of this chapter.

# CHAPTER 10
## Man's Real "Free Choice" in this World – in Two Words

In this chapter the clarity that we've gained 'comes to a head' as we get a glimpse of what man's free choice in this world really involves: his equally balanced ability to *follow through* on what he knows in his heart to be true or to *ignore* his own heart's knowledge.

# CHAPTER 11
## Applying the Foundational Axioms in a Practical Way

Turn here if what you seek is how the knowledge of all these "big" ideas can help make your life any easier. This Chapter outlines a practical tool of how you can utalize the knowledge gained thus far to your benefit during difficult times: it demonstrates to you how you can extricate yourself from any trying situation in the most positive way.

# AUTHOR'S PREFACE

For as long as I can remember, I've always loved life.

I enjoy the thrill and challenge of having *to accomplish* something.

Throughout my childhood and teenage years, I invested time and effort to accomplish what I thought was "supposed to be" accomplished, whether it was to be the strongest fighter among the boys, the best ballplayer, the best singer (I wasn't very successful at any of those); or the funniest in class, the most animated, a good speech giver (I was better at those). Later, when my interests shifted from boyish, selfish accomplishments to more altruistic, "spiritual" goals, I tried to become a *medakdek b'mitzvos* (a most devoted *mitzvah* adherent), a good learner, a unique and respected individual within the community, etc. Yet for many, many years, and up until recently, it still remained unclear to me: "What exactly *was* supposed to be accomplished in life?"

Today, after years of searching, sacrificing, and yes, even pain, I feel that through Hashem's Great *Rachamim* and *Chasadim* (Compassion and Love), I have merited a level of clarity in discovering what the real goal of our lives is. I've found an explanation that I feel comfortable and 'at peace' with; one that makes sense and 'brings together' most all of the varying ideas that our holy religion professes are goals for us to achieve. One that answers the question of what we need to focus on most in our lives and what we really *are* supposed to accomplish.

In keeping with the dictum of *"Lilmod U'L'Lamed"* – learn it first for yourself, and then go and teach it to others – I now feel that I want to share my clarity with others who may also be searching for what I was searching for; to give them the answers that I have found; to define what it *is* exactly that we are expected to accomplish during these limited years of the beautiful, amazing and magnificent life that we are granted here in this world. Even if I can't present the answer here in its full, unabridged form, at least I can try to present it in some succinct way.

I sincerely hope that you, the reader, will benefit from the clarity you acquire and will come to appreciate it as I do – with tremendous gratitude to Hashem for having been granted these understandings. Perhaps you will come to challenge some of the connection of Torah ideas I have cited which I have understood to be implicit. I would welcome such deliberation – as Chazal say, Torah is only acquired through group [interaction] (Berachos 63b). And then together, we can endeavor to clarify what it is that Hashem, our G-d, expects of us – even today, at 'the end of days', when we are lacking in the overt channels of *Ruach Hakodesh* and *Nevuah* (Prophesy) to be able to hear from Him explicitly what it is exactly that we need to do.

May the *zchus* (merit) of us yearning and searching together be accepted by Hashem and give Him *nachas* (pleasure and satisfaction), when He sees that His children who have 'lost their direction' in the *galus* (exile) are trying nonetheless to 'find their way back toward Him'. May He *reveal* to us very soon the Reality of *His True Presence* – the Source of all *Da'as* (Knowledge and Clarity), as well as the Source of everything else in this magnificent life of ours that we so enjoy. May the revelation of that Presence – that is really *always here with us* and that we have believed in and waited for throughout this treacherously long *galus* (exile) – come speedily in our days, *b'mheira v'yameinu*, Amen.

# PREFACE:
## How to Use This Book

Did you notice that the title says "to *Use*", and not "to *Read*" this book?

That's because reading and **gaining "information" is only half of the battle; to apply and benefit from these concepts of** *hashkafah* (Jewish wisdom, guidance, and outlook on life that have been passed down throughout the generations), **you must** *act*[1].

This book offers you a shortcut to years of studying Jewish *hashkafos* and searching for their sources. In the upcoming pages, you will find the original sources for many of the concepts that govern our lives. Still, no sources or deeper insights can improve your spiritual life if all you do is read them. You must put the principles into action.

## From Study to Practice

Our holy Sages have taught us that it takes 40 days to change

---

[1] *"Lo hamedrash hu ha'ikar elah hama'aseh"* – "the study is not the main [goal], rather the action" (*Pirkei Avos* 1-17).

an accustomed behavior pattern[2], or to develop a new one. I sincerely believe that if each time you read, you begin to apply practically what you've learned to your daily outlook and actions, just a little at a time, you *will* get results.

If you do not have the time available to read this book in order, nonetheless make sure that you have ample time *to absorb* the concepts.

You will discover as you encounter the explanations for the foundational concepts, that they are not merely theoretical, but also offer a way to relate to life in practical terms. Give yourself time to absorb this knowledge. In order to facilitate absorption of the ideas, the setting of the actual 'handbook of axioms' is situated between interludes of a give-and-take dialogue. The reader will find that sometimes unspoken questions regarding a previous chapter are articulated in the dialogue, and that the answers given can help to better understand the principles that were previously introduced.

To further help absorption, rereading a chapter three or four times will give you a stronger retention[3]. You will begin to view daily Jewish life in a different light, and you will be able to set more effective priorities toward reaching your personal life's goal.

Our Sages (*Chazal*) tell us that the best way to undertake a learning project is to focus each time on a small amount[4] and

---

[2] *Tzetel Katan* from Rebbe Elimelech of Lizensk *z"l, os tes zayin*.
[3] Eiruvin 54b: "Rebbe Eliezer said: A person is obligated to review for his student four times… If this was so by Ahron, who learned from the teachings of Moshe, and Moshe [learned] from the teachings of Hashem (G-d) [and yet he still needed to review a new piece of Oral Torah *She'be'al Peh* four times], most certainly [it is so (needed to review four times) when] a regular person [learns] from a regular person."
[4] *Vayikra Rabbah, Parsha yud-tes, os beis*.

put it into practice,[5] and by doing so we will better reach our ultimate goal. So it's suggested to just read one chapter – or even one section within a chapter – at a time, and then find a way to put into action what you just read. Don't wait until you finish the whole book to apply what you've learned. Firstly, it's better not to wait in applying what you learn; and also, you're likely to forget valuable insights and practical applications you'd gained from reading the initial chapters. So read, then do, then read some more. We can learn this art of focused concentration from a young child just beginning to walk, who thinks only about the step in front of him, making sure it's balanced and secure, while not thinking about any of the upcoming steps at all[6].

## Suggestions for Partial Reading

**If your time for reading is very limited**, start with Chapters 2, 5 and 6 which include most all of the foundational axiomatic concepts. These principles are the foundations upon which everything else is built, and will enable you to be able to understand and to retain the summary which is presented in the beginning of Chapter 9. [Alternatively, you may choose to spend your limited time in reading the Introduction – which explains *why* the ideas in this work are so important for our generation today – at which point you might find that you have *more* time than you originally thought you had to invest in clarifying these ideas for yourself.]

---

[5]*Mishna* Pirkei Avos (3-9): "*Kol shema'asav merubim mai'chachmuso, chachmuso miskayemes*" – Rabbenu Yonah explains this Mishna as specifically relating good advice as to how to retain the knowledge that one has gained through intellectual study: he should accept upon himself from the beginning of his learning that whatever he learns from the *Chachamim* (Torah Sages) from now on, he will *immediately put into action*.

[6]*Sefer Yismach Yisroel, Parshas Shlach, os aleph*, quotes the teaching of Rebbe Simcha Bunim of Parshisch *z"l* that it is necessary for every Jewish person not to ponder and think about what will be afterward, just to focus on the moment that he is standing in.

If you are presently in a life-trying situation, you might find it most effective to 'skip' to the formula quoted in Chapter 11, and then, only afterwards, delve more deeply into understanding the specific concepts that apply. As you do, you'll likely find that your understanding will have been made clearer by the practical steps that you'd previously taken during the trying moments.

Perhaps you're currently concerned with building your level of *emunah* (belief and trust in G-d), especially in a world where there's so much atheism and doubt – then go to Chapter 4.

Or maybe you want to focus on your personal relationship with Hashem (G-d), and how you can develop it to a greater degree – then go to Chapters 7 and 8.

If you feel that you're presently unable to invest much time at all, you may choose to concentrate just on the summary of the foundational axioms themselves, presented at the beginning and end of Chapter 9.

## Identify the Source

A large part of being able to gain clarity in regard to life's purpose is to verify the written sources on the topic in a clear way. Don't feel pressured to have to absorb everything found in this book all at once; read at your own pace and according to your own style of study – but just make sure that you know where the written source is, and that you understand it to the best of your ability.

So much confusion in regard to the Jewish life-outlook and *hashkafah* is caused by respectable people saying: "I *heard* that you're supposed to...". The next time you hear someone say "I *heard* that..." ask him: "Where is it *written?*" If he can actually answer where it says what he claims, it is probably worthwhile for you to check it out and see if it is actually written the way he said it was, before you base any act in your life upon it. Unfortunately, the nature of human beings lends itself to quoting and applying ideas inexactly or even mistakenly, and it's often necessary to exert extra effort to clarify exactly what was being transmitted. The spoken word can also be deceiving if a single line was taken out of context. In contrast, what is penned in the form of the written word and was 'signed upon' by a universally accepted leader of the Jewish people, is a guarantee that he was careful and exacting in his words; and we can also easily locate the context in which he wrote his words. Therefore, it is specifically the written word that we need to rely upon heavily in order to gain clarity in regard to our understanding of the Jewish life-outlook.

Once you know what the written source is for any given *hashkafic* concept, you hold an invaluable key that can open the door to a new understanding on life. No one will be able to claim to you anymore that "It doesn't say that anywhere" or to argue with you that it says differently. You will just show him where it is written. No one will be able to confuse you anymore by claiming something that they heard someone tell them, which in reality the source doesn't say. You will just look it up together in the written source. No one will be able to add their 'personal interpretation' (or guess) anymore in trying to influence you to act in some way that you were never expected to act in the first place according to the Torah — because you now hold the original source in your hand[7].

---

[7] *"Kol ha'omer davar b'shem omro maivie geulah l'olam"* — "Anyone who says something in the name of its initiator (the first source of the saying) brings *geulah* (redemption to the world) [Pirkei Avos 6-6] — because he causes life in this world to become more orderly and corrected; whereas if a person quotes something inexactly, he is in essence causing life in this world to become more disorganized and confusing — and thus *galus* (exile) to remain in the world.

Having the original source with the actual written words before you also gives you the opportunity to learn them again and again until you fully understand the intent of the idea or concept. Even if you don't fully understand some of the sources, you now have the opportunity to turn to a proficient *hashkafic* authority to explain it to you in a way that you can understand, rather than to rely in regard to life questions, on the well-meaning interpretation of a one-time acquaintance.

If you "use" this book to apply these most foundational concepts in a practical and "hands-on" way to your daily life, and you use it also to access the source writings for what we believe in as the Jewish nation is the purpose of our lives, I have no doubt that not only can your individual lives change for the better from the clarity you've gained, but *also all of our lives* can change for the better with Hashem's help — being that we really are *all* connected and share one collective goal.

Thus together, may we be able to emerge from this fog of confusion and *galus* (exile) into the clear shine of clarity and *geulah* (redemption), speedily in our days, Amen.

# INTRODUCTION

## Why is this Message – Getting Clarity on Life's Purpose – so Relevant Today?

As religious Jews today, we live in communities that are often comprised of **contrasting elements of two very different worlds:** Pre-WWII Europe and Post-WWII America.

A great change transpired in Jewish history in the aftermath of WWII. In addition to everything else that it caused, WWII created a drastic shift in the central Jewish population centers. This dynamic often goes unmentioned, and indeed might seem hardly worth bringing up in light of WWII's other devastating consequences, including the loss of six million Jewish lives *Hy"d*. Yet today this factor is having a profound effect on the educational approach for the younger generation. Whereas before WWII the major Jewish population centers were primarily located in Eastern Europe (for *Ashkenazim*), and remained, to a large extent, similar to the traditional *shtetl* (Jewish village) setting; after WWII, the population centers, which had emigrated to America, had largely lost the feel of the pre-war European *shtetl*.

Being that the external surroundings in the "*naiya land*" (new land) of America no longer resembled those of Europe, it was inevitable that the children who would grow up there would no longer experience the same degree of "living Judaism" – part and parcel of "the air inhaled" in the pre-war *shtetlach* – that their parents had. Of course, there were numerous communities even in America who invested painstaking effort in trying to preserve the *shtetl*'s "closed-setting" feel. Many surviving religious communities adopted the approach of "*insulation*" – to "build walls" and insulate their offspring from secular infiltration – in attempt to ensure that the legacy of Jewish values retain its authenticity for the new generation in the face of its new challenges. However, unlike in Europe, the American non-Jewish population wasn't living in a totally separate section of town or across a river anymore; now they were living "down the block" – at the furthest – and their lifestyle and customs were openly displayed for every Jewish boy and girl to observe whenever they went outside. Accordingly, the upcoming generation's experience of Judaism was inevitably influenced, at least to some degree, by the surrounding American culture.

At the beginning of this period (the 1950's), that influence was not terribly threatening. Aside from baseball and hotdogs – which could somehow be "repackaged" in a kosher form – the mainstream secular values of those years didn't seem much at odds with the principles of Torah. Family values, the work ethic, and pursuit of knowledge and study were held in high esteem. Loyalty, and trustworthiness in business dealings, were values that even the secular culture of the time embraced. Under such conditions the approach of "insulation" proved to be a valid option, and Hashem blessed the self-sacrifice and dedicated efforts of the survivors, to be able for the most part to raise their children with a sense of appreciation for the same lifestyle that they themselves had experienced when growing up in the *shtetlach* of pre-war Europe.

But then came the counter-culture of the 1960's, which to everyone's shock expanded in the 1970's to become the mainstream culture (possibly because of the great antagonism that people felt from the perceived purposelessness of exposing young Americans to life-threatening situations for the benefit of the South Vietnamese people). Then, for the next 30 years, the path of secular values continued to change drastically. The previously accepted etiquette of societal morals shifted steadily over time: The importance of raising a family turned into a creed of not building one – due to the investment of time and effort that it required. The significance of the work ethic and of applying oneself sincerely to one's job, turned into the heroic approbation of the underachiever. The esteemed respect for knowledge and serious study turned into its disregard – the advent of Wikipedia making the need to access knowledge from a living individual, archaic. The axiomatic principles of loyalty and trustworthiness in business dealings gave way to cutthroat competition even for just a few dollars. Over the years these and other secular overtures slowly seeped their way even into the most insulated Jewish communities of post-war America, especially among the youth.

To add "insult to injury", advances in technology over the last 25 years have delivered much of the above-mentioned secular "progress" right into the midst of the insulated camp. Whereas before, a religious person tempted by the draw of secularism, would at least have to go "out of the camp," to the other side of town, to find what he was looking for, now he could easily access whatever he was seeking while still in the midst of the "insulated" camp, just by locking his own door.

Today, likely due to the combined influence of all the factors mentioned above, we have unfortunately become witness to the increased number of stories of "falling souls" from among young members of the Jewish community. Is there anything that we can possibly do to reverse the trend that threatens to uproot much of what our fathers and all the previous generations of faithful Jews gave their lives in order to preserve?

## Experiential versus Conceptual

To answer this question, the original distinction made, between those parts of our community that drew from the elements of Pre-WWII Europe and those parts that draw from the elements of Post-WWII America, becomes criticial.

In pre-war Europe, the majority of Jewish youth growing up in strongly religious communities *were able to absorb a positive connection* to their Judaism. This took place almost by "osmosis"; the lifestyle and the "feel in the air" of what Judaism represented was contagious. In such times it wasn't necessary to discuss Judaism's answers to the existential questions of life, nor to assert as to why it had the "right" approach – as opposed to the world's other religions – because to add any logical explanations to *Bubbie's* "gut knowledge" that "*Der Aibeshter vet helfen*" was superfluous and, at times, even detrimental. There was never any question about the validity of *Bubbie's emunah* (steadfast belief) in the first place, so why even raise a question concerning *something that had already been clearly established for everyone?* During those years, the general approach was "*better not to ask*" rather than endeavor "to find out what to answer the *apikorus* (agnostic)".[1] "*Emunah pshuta*" (simple

---

[1] Pirkei Avos 2:14.

and unquestioning belief) was strongly ingrained and there was no reason to bring up potentially confusing queries when one didn't have to.

Unfortunately, today that reality has greatly changed. In post-war America, the majority of Jewish youth growing up even in strongly religious communities *do not automatically absorb a positive connection* to their Judaism by "osmosis". They do not tangibly sense the feel of excitement in the air when a Shabbos or Yom Tov arrives. Nor do they feel the Jewish lifestyle bubbling around them every time they step out of the door of their home, like it might have been in Europe. Whereas in pre-war Europe, the internal connection of a young Jewish soul *was re-inforced* by the **experiential knowledge** he absorbed from his surroundings, a young Jewish soul in contemporary America, in general, *does not have access to that experience*. Whereas in Europe it was superfluous and unnecessary to engage in developing a **conceptual knowledge** of Judaism, in America *it is the only real alternative* toward enhancing *a non-shtetl-exposed soul* with a positive connection to his Judaism.

Generally speaking, every committed religious Jew today has internalized his connection to his Judaism in **one of these two** ways. Either he was fortunate enough that his upbringing and exposure to religious Judaism included a strong influence from elements of pre-war Europe in order to afford him an *experiential knowledge* of Judaism; or it was predominantly influenced from elements of post-war America, and he absorbed a *conceptual knowledge* of Judaism. This contradistinction has become a source of confusion in many present-day communities.

One fortunate enough to have had a childhood where he absorbed an *experiential knowledge* of Judaism, will likely be of the opinion that a conceptual knowledge of Judaism is unnecessary. He sees things through the lens of his own experience, and to the best of *his* knowledge and experience, a conceptual perception of Judaism is only superfluous and can sometimes even cause harm.

Conversely, one whose background necessitated him to strengthen himself through seeking a *conceptual knowledge* of Judaism (such as a 'baal teshuva', 'modern', etc.) is likely to feel that a conceptual knowledge of Judaism is an absolute necessity. He likewise sees things through the lens of his own experience, and to the best of *his* knowledge and experience, a conceptual perception of Judaism is crucial today for anyone to be able to come to a positive connection with his Judaism.

Two opposite approaches: both correct – *for each individual.* The problem begins when we generalize, and one attempts to superimpose his personal experience and approach upon others who are neither similar to, nor have had the same experience as he. Then, the well-meaning approach, which was intended to help and not to harm, can actually end up causing detrimental consequences to the intended beneficiaries. The confusion intensifies, when these two contrasting individuals – each of whom is convinced that his approach is the 'right one for everybody' – buy homes in the same community, live next door to each other, send their children to the same schools, etc.

## Teaching to Swim Outside of Natural Habitat

Perhaps we can better understand this issue by comparing teaching our children to feel positive about their Judaism to teaching young fish how to swim. A fish can learn how to swim in one of two ways: either in a natural body of water or in a fish tank. Teaching children about Judaism in an *experiential* way is similar to teaching fish how to swim in a natural body of water – in their natural habitat. Teaching children about Judaism in a *conceptual* way is like teaching fish how to swim in a tank – a constructed, "man-made" habitat. While one may assert that fish swim better if they learn initially in their natural habitat rather than in a man-made one, no one will argue that learning to swim in a "man-made" tank is not called swimming.

What is crucial to understand is that many of today's youth – *even those growing up within "insulated" communities* – do not always have the "luxury" of accessing the *experiential* approach. For one of a myriad of possible reasons, they did not internalize a true, inner, and positive connection to Judaism as their teachers, parents, friends, or even siblings might have. For some reason, they simply did not succeed in learning how to "swim" in the natural body of water. That being the case, the only remaining option available for them to develop a positive connection to their Judaism and to learn how to "swim" is to *"build them tanks"*. **We have to take the "conceptual route".** We need now to make them aware of the existential questions, to show them how beautifully and accurately Judaism answers each one, and to allow them through their own processing to realize how valuable a positive connection to their Judaism is to their life. *This is what will provide them with the "water" they need in order to begin to "flex their muscles" and to nurture their own positive connection to Judaism for the rest of their lives.*

Should a staunch believer in the "experiential approach" then counter by saying: "But this is not what went on in previous generations!" – "*af atah emor lo*", you need to answer him according to the deeper logic that is hidden *within his own question*.

His assertion: "This is not an approach that was present in previous generations" – is essentially true. But to reach the even deeper truth, you must bring him to follow the logic of his own question. "Yes," you must answer, "that is true. But *what is the reason* that this approach was not present or utilized in previous generations? The answer is because in all those generations of pre-war Europe, the "conceptual approach" was *unnecessary*. The tangible experience of the surroundings filled the spiritual storehouses of a Jewish soul with more than what it needed." Since such an approach was not essential, and since at times it might have even detracted, it was understood then that it was better to avoid it completely.

"But today that reality has changed; even if it hasn't changed for you personally — because of the inner storehouses of experience that *you* merited to receive and that you are able to continuously draw from even today — that doesn't mean that those who don't possess such a rich inner supply of experience, or those who have never had the chance to be exposed to the experience that you had, should be prohibited to use the conceptual approach, which is a valid Torah alternative. If you wish to prohibit someone who needs it from gaining a conceptual knowledge of Judaism, it is equivalent to expecting a fish to learn how to swim while *both* outside of a natural body of water and *also* outside of a tank. (And you know what the result is when that takes place.)"

## Conceptual Becomes a "Prerequisite" to Experiential

This is why the study of basic Jewish *hashkafah* (life-outlook) is so essential today. The experiential knowledge which was available to the youth of pre-war Europe filled their internal reserves with a positive feeling about Judaism even without any conceptual explanations; however, this is not the reality today. The essential knowledge that Hashem Cares about each and every Jewish soul and Loves them to such an extent that His entire Intent in creation is just to Give them the Greatest Level of Good – a concept woven into the fabric of Jewish belief, which was passed down by "osmosis" for so many generations – unfortunately stands today with a *big* question mark in the minds of many of the youth. This core message of Judaism is now threatened to become forgotten by many young Jews today if it is not taught to them explicitly.

Yet it is also not sufficient to resolve the issue by teaching young people the conceptual principles alone. While young Jews who question whether Hashem really cares about them need first to see conceptually that this is truly a tenet of Torah, they need *also* to make it an experiential reality. Once they digest the truth of the concepts, they need to test them in the "laboratory" of their daily lives. For if the ideas remain only in their minds only in a theoretical and abstract way, we have not yet accomplished the goal of giving them the tools they need to build a positive and real relationship with Hashem. Indeed, the "conceptual route" is in essence but *a means* to help them reach the necessary goal of the inner, experiential knowledge.

Therefore, if as we teach these intellectual concepts, we *simultaneously* emphasize their practical application and we give them the ability to attain also the experiential knowledge they so lack, we can be successful – with Hashem's help – to arouse a new wave of enthusiasm for maintaining a true and fulfilling Jewish lifestyle among the youth. For example, if we encourage them to actually speak about *what is concerning them* to Hashem, to *daven* (pray) to Hashem in a way that creates a connection, and to follow the rules that we have passed down as to how to make their prayers likely to be answered, this truly causes them to begin *to experience* results. Sensing Hashem answering them in a tangible way then imbues them with the *experiential* knowledge of their initially learned *conceptual* truths, which compensates for their initial lack on the experiential level. Only then can they truly acquire a *heart knowledge* that Hashem Really Does Care *about them*.

This combination of personal *experiential knowledge*, together with a clear intellectual and conceptual understanding, can foster within them a strong, positive connection with Judaism which can hold up even in the face of all the non-spiritual experiences which encircle them today. To return to our *mashal* (parable), by giving them the 'Big Picture' of Judaism we build them a "fish tank", and by emphasizing the importance of practical application we encourage them to begin "swimming" on their own, enabling them to attain a firm, inner attachment to Judaism, comparable to the once available "natural bodies of water" that were widespread in the *shtetl* of pre-war Europe.

It is the hope and prayer of the author, that by presenting the most basic Torah principles and their holy sources in a logical and orderly manner, together with tools of how to utilize this knowledge practically, that many more young Jews will come to internally embrace the beliefs of their fathers; will sense Hashem's ongoing Support and His answering of their prayers; and will begin to feel proud of the crown of Judaism which they carry. This , in turn, can then bring us to that day when the knowledge of Hashem and His Goodness will be tangible throughout the entire world, like water that covers the entire ocean, speedily in our days, Amen.

# It's All for the GOOD?

*It was a dark and overcast night when my eyes locked with a pair of shining blue, familiar ones.*

*"Yisrael, how are you?!" I instinctively exclaimed to a student of mine who I hadn't seen for a long time.*

*"Rav! It's great to see you! And how are you and your family getting along back in Israel?"*

*"It's a great merit to be living in Israel and thank G-d all are well. But tell me, what are you doing nowadays?"*

*"Rav, I am a businessman and thank G-d I can tell you that I'm able to keep set times for Torah study every single day. I even tear myself away from the office two afternoons a week to go and hear a class of in-depth talmud study. While you are in the class you "feel it" – the intensity, the excitement – but then when it's over, it's hard to get that feeling back until the next class; which comes only a few days later or the next week. And you know, it's just not enough to carry me over anymore, and things are becoming harder and harder. Many times I find myself yearning to hear those Torah classes about hashkafah (Jewish outlook on the world) again, the ones that I heard when I was learning in Israel. That's something which could carry a person over; the sense of strength that comes from knowing that everything you're doing fits into a 'big picture' plan of life is tremendously motivating. For instance, I've learned about "the purpose of a Jew's life" – but if I could really internalize and understand how to apply the 'big picture' outlook in a practical way, I'd be a different person. And Rav, I'm telling you, it's not only me."*

Dialogue  1

This was not the first time I heard such words from one of the students who was desiring to review hashkafah. This time, however, seeing Yisrael's sincere yearning for a summary of the Jewish outlook on the world touches something inside of me and slightly jars open a door of consideration.

"I can see that people could use review on 'the purpose of life'" I began. "I often hear people arguing vehemently as they try to formulate their own opinions regarding questions of the Jewish outlook on such topics that are already discussed and answered explicitly in Torah literature. Since they're unaware of these sources – or that there even are sources – they just forcefully argue, and don't even reach a satisfying conclusion." I lament, as Yisrael looks on, engaged.

"I'm not even talking about those types of questions that result from a difference of opinion between acclaimed Torah leaders throughout the generations. I'm talking about the Torah's basic foundational principles, which are indisputable because of their universally accepted sources."

"INDISPUTABLE opinions of Jewish outlook?" Yisrael interjects.

"Yes," I say. "These are basic axioms that every Torah-knowledgeable Jewish person in the world would agree upon, and which should not be cause for any type of confusion or argument. And yet they are, because people are unaware of the source answers to their questions, which are often found in the deeper Torah writings."

"So, Rav, why wouldn't you just write a book that will teach people these axioms? That way you'll take away people's confusion and empower them with the knowledge of these foundational principles. It should not only include a description of the ideas, but their sources as well, so that the readers will see that the sources are accepted by all and are, like you say... indisputable."

I like the idea, but feel hesitant. "Do you really think there'd be an interest?"

"Are you kidding? I know I'd be interested. Let me already give you my bracha (blessing): May Hashem give you the Siyata D'Shmaya (Heavenly assistance) that you will need to write out the axioms of Jewish belief in a clear and orderly way, so that I, together with many more Jewish souls, can have the opportunity to gain clarity and understand the purpose of our lives!"

**In This Chapter:**
> What does the word "axiom" mean?
> Why are axioms so important?
> Is there one axiom that is *objective* and applicable to everyone?

# It All Starts with Your Axioms

Clarifying the purpose of your life is one of the most vital things you can do. It rewards you with a priceless sense of meaning and a goal to strive for throughout life. But in order to properly clarify life's purpose, you have to first *verify your axioms*. Our axioms form the basis for our understanding of everything in life.

## What are Axioms?

Axioms are those most fundamental principles that you never talk about. They are the accepted 'givens' that people assume from the start, the truth of which become self-evident as a person continues to live with them.

For example, a child may ask his parents "How did the world get here?' or "Where was I born?", but under normal circumstances he would never ask "Am I alive?" The reason is **axioms form the basis for our understanding** because its truth is self-evident to him through his very existence.

Another example of an accepted truism is when a parent asks a child who is holding an object to put it down. The child would never refuse by saying "But if I let go, maybe it will fall up into the sky". The reality of gravity is accepted axiomatically by all living beings on this Earth. Its truth is apparent in every human being's daily function in the world.

**it is not very apparent to us why we are here**

In regard to the purpose of our lives, it is not very apparent to us why we are here, what's our purpose? In order to get the clarity we're looking for, first we need to begin with an axiom: something that is a fundamental truism, the truth of which should become self-evident to us as we continue to live with it.

The problem in finding that first axiom in regard to the purpose of our lives is that the scope of human experience is so vast that it is virtually impossible for us to discover the *absolute starting point* "for everything". The sum of all human experience includes all the experiences on the face of this Earth, as well as those throughout the universe and even beyond that, on to spiritual experiences. The physical universe alone is so vast that we cannot even define its outermost parameters – it seems to us like it has no beginning and no end. So how can we ever determine an *objective starting point* within an unlimited reality?

## Choosing a Starting Point

Yet our minds are finite, and so, as human beings, we *must* have a "starting point" in order to begin to think about anything.

Precisely because it is almost impossible for us to be able to determine the real, absolute starting point for "everything", often this "starting point" is chosen by people arbitrarily. It is essentially an *unproven* assumption that one adopts, "just because" we have finite minds and we *have to have* a starting point. They may then proceed to build an entire cosmology based upon this first assumption when the first assumption itself is only something that they've accepted without any proof at all.

For example, the Copernican principle (that the Earth is not the center of the universe) is the foundation for all studies regarding the Big Bang theory (which involve even construction of huge particle accelerators costing billions of dollars). Yet the Copernican principle itself has never been proven and is just an assumption that is used implicitly in many theories of modern physics.

Truth be told, it is unwise and irresponsible for anyone to make important, life-long decisions that will affect him and his family, without first having verified for himself whether the axiomatic foundation upon which he is basing a large part of his life is true or is not. Just as we only build our life around such physical axioms that prove themselves through the reality of our lives, so too we should only build our life around such spiritual axioms that can prove themselves through the reality of our lives.

## Spiritual Axioms

It is challenging to verify the spiritual axioms, as the only way to properly do so is by means of *one's personal experience*.

Because of this, many of the spiritual axioms that are accepted by the world at large are *subjective*. Someone choses an arbitrary starting point just to be able to start "from somewhere"[1],

---

[1] Only when two people begin with similar axioms will they be able to engage in a debate and joint study of a topic that will yield any productive conclusions. The Rambam tells us explicitly (Introduction to the Explanation of the Mishnayos *Seder Zeraim*): "This issue is clear, that any two people, being at an equal level in intellect, in examination and in the knowledge of the axioms from which the logic[al conclusions] are derived, [there] will not fall disagreement between them in their logic at all; and if it fell, it will be minimal." In order for two individuals to reach an agreeable conclusion, they must first have the knowledge of the agreed upon axioms from which the conclusions

and then large numbers of people accept this "starting point" without ever having tried at all to verify the axiom's validity *through their own personal experience*.

**there is an objective "starting point"** Traditional Jewish belief teaches that there is an *objective* "starting point" that applies equally to everyone and everything in the world. It is *not* subjective and was *not* chosen arbitrarily. It is one that *can* be verified through each individual's own experience. Once we begin to live with this axiom, it is one that *does* prove itself the more a person continues to live with it[2].

What is this absolute "starting point" that we have passed down, and how does it "prove itself" through our individual experience?

---

### Chapter Quick Points

> Axioms form the basis for our understanding of everything in life.

> Very often people adopt a non-proven (subjective) axiom as the basis for their approach to life.

> According to traditional Jewish belief, there is an absolute (objective) axiom that applies equally to everyone and everything in the world.

---

are subsequently derived. The Rambam's words also imply that if any two people *do not* begin with the same axioms — even if their intellectual and logical capabilities are similar — they *will not* reach the same conclusion. It follows from this, that if you ever debate with someone over any issue that involves a verification of truth, if your intent is to reach any sort of consensus in your conclusion, *make sure* beforehand that you and your opponent's axiomatic starting-points are the same. See source in Appendix I.
[2]See Chapter 4.

**In This Chapter:**

> What does "Hashem" mean?

> Who is Hashem – Really?

> What can we fully grasp about Hashem?

# The First Basic Axiom: Who is Hashem?

According to traditional Jewish belief, the *objective* starting point of everything is: "Hashem". The Torah *starts off:* "In the beginning, **Hashem** created heaven and earth" (1:1). G-d's *first words* to the Jewish people when giving them the Torah were: "**I am Hashem,** your G-d". Maimonides, when enumerating the mitzvos, *begins with* the very first mitzva as being: "Know that there exists a **First Cause (i.e. Hashem)** and He Brings into existence everything which exists".

This is the objective "starting point" that we have passed down in traditional Jewish belief. It is what *was revealed to us*[3] as being the true spiritual starting point for everything. It is something we would have never been able to guess in this world of ours which seems from our perspective to be endless; it is not something that someone "just chose" arbitrarily. It *is* something that can be

---

[3] Although the "starting point" was told to us and not discovered on our own [see Rashi Devorim 4-35: "When Hashem gave the Torah, He opened up for them seven heavens... and they saw that He is [the only Source] One"], that does not take away from its validity. Since the rule of a valid axiom is that it be verifiable within the realm of our ongoing life experience, once it becomes clear to us through experience that it is true, it makes no difference how we initially acquired the information. This can be exemplified to someone who has just downloaded a complex computer program. Although he has the option of trying to discover the workings of the program on his own through trial and error, if the program developer were to inform him of all the functions and how to activate them, the fact that he did not come to it on his own would make no difference in terms of the truth of the information, as long as it actually works.

clearly verified *through one's personal experience*[4]. But before we begin to test or to apply this *first axiom*, we must first understand who *Hashem* is.

## Hashem's "Name"

The word "Hashem" literally means "The Name". It is a reference to the particular Name of G-d that was revealed to Moses in Egypt[5]. It is referred to as "The Name", alluding to the fact that it may only be contemplated in thought, and not pronounced[6]. Although we are not permitted to enunciate the letters of "The Name" of G-d, and only refer to it as "Hashem" or "Ado-noy" (our Master), the actual letters themselves hold the key to their meaning. The etymological root of the letters pertains to the Hebrew verb of "being" or "existing"[7]. Therefore, whenever we contemplate or refer to the "The Name" or to "Hashem", our intent is really to describe G-d as *"the One Who brings all that we know of into being*[8]*"*.

Yet even this description, while sufficient to fulfill our basic, required level of relating to G-d through our prayers[9], is limited by

---

[4]See Chapter 4.

[5]Shmos 3-15:"This is My Name forever, and this is how I will be remembered for generation [after] generation".

[6]Kiddushin 71a:"It is written (Shmos 3-15):"This is My Name 'forever' " [the spelling of the Hebrew word "forever" (*l'olam*), is spelled in the Torah with the same letters as the Hebrew word "to hide" (*l'alem*); meaning to teach us, that the word *l'olam* itself that was told to Moshe hinted at the requirement to:] — 'keep it hidden', (as *l'olam* is spelled. Says *Hakadosh Baruch Hu*: Not the way that I am written (i.e. That My Name is written), I am read (is My Name pronounced); in writing [I am called with the Name of] *Yud, Hey*; in reading [by the Name of] *Aleph Daled*".

[7]The Hebrew words for the verb of "being" are: *Hayah* (was), *Hoveh* (is), and *Yehiyeh* (will be) — all of whose letters are included in the spelling of Hashem's Name.

[8]"Because this Name corroborates [the fact] that anything that exists, exists. …It is the Foundation of the essence of every existence and its reality" (*Sefer Ginas Egoz*, quoted in *Shelah Hakadosh*, "*Bais Hashem*", paragraph beginning *Od nevaer*).

[9]The words *Hayah* (was), *Hoveh* (is), and *Yehiyeh* (will be) are actually the intent that one is required to have when mentioning Hashem's name in prayer (*Orach Chaim, siman* 5-1. [According to the Vilna Gaon, this specific intent is only a necessary requirement when reciting the first verse of *kriyas Shema* (*Mishna Brurah, seif katan* 3)]).

our finite human perspective, and does not fully encapsulate His *True Reality*. It is only from our limited human perspective that we refer to G-d in terms of the attribute of "Being" and *"the One Who brings all that we know of into existence"*. There is yet an even higher and more inclusive conception of Hashem that pertains to His True Reality.[10]

**this description is limited by our finite human perspective**

In His True Reality, "Hashem", infinitely transcends the description of "just" being *the One Who brings all that we know of into being*; His True Reality is **Infinity Itself**.

## Ain Sof *Baruch Hu* —The **Infinite One** *Blessed be He*

The Kabbalists teach[11] that the only reference to Hashem that we can use to describe His True Essence, is *"Ain Sof"* — literally, *No (i.e. beyond) Description*[12] — *"Baruch Hu"*, Blessed be He. That is to say, the only *real* description for Hashem is: "*No possible* description", "*No possible* limitation", "*No possible* encompassing articulation or reference"[13]. Any word or description that we may express already implies some sort of border or limitation. Since we are finite beings and our minds can only grasp finite concepts, all of our

---

[10] And therefore, whenever we learn or talk about Hashem, and think about Him as "being the One Who brings everything that we know of into existence", it is always with the understanding that this is the way that Hashem *wants us* to relate to Him — since this is the extent of what *we* are capable of. Yet we ourselves need always to be aware that the "Real Reality" of Hashem which is Infinite is far beyond anything that we can ever grasp or fathom.

[11] "The First aspect [and the First Cause of all creation] is [the Reality of] the *Ain Sof* Who Is [exemplified to us as] Totally, Simple Light [i.e. Life-Force] without any form of utensils or picture [that define or contain] at all, *chas v'shalom*. And This, The *Ain Sof* , He Is The True, Ultimate Source of Emanation Who brought forth all of the worlds" (*Kisvei Ha'Ari z"l Sha'ar Hahakdomos, Sha'ar Aleph, hakdomah daled, daf zayin*).

[12] In *Tefilas Eliyahu*, Eliyahu Hanavi *z"l* says: "There is no thought that can grasp any aspect of You at all" (*Hakdomah L'Tikunei Zohar*, 17a).

[13] "*There is no speech or word [which gives definition] with which to speak about Him*, and there is no concept or intellect that can grasp Him" (*Sefer Leshem, Shvo, V'Achlama, Igulim V'Yosher, Anaf Aleph, os aleph*).

words and communications necessarily relate to finite existences. We can therefore not use *our limited concepts* in defining Hashem. Hashem's *True Existence* is so great and so beyond our capabilities to grasp, that any description we could ever conceive of is already limiting of Him and is therefore, untrue.

Were we to attempt to imagine the "Reality of Hashem" as He *really* is, we'd need to imagine Him as being without any limitation or description or reference[14] — which is impossible for us to imagine. The Kabbalists therefore tell us that the most accurate way for us to perceive of Hashem is as *Existence* — but beyond any specific description that we can fathom. We can come to know for sure that *Ain Sof* Baruch Hu *Exists* — but we cannot truly encompass in our minds *His Essence*[15]. His true Essence is the Source Life-giving force itself, the Source Energy for everything; although we can grasp that it Exists, we cannot grasp what its Essence truly is[16].

Although we are finite beings with finite concepts, and from our limited perspective the greatest way we can imagine "Hashem" is as *"the One Who brings all that we know of into being"*, Hashem's Ultimate and True Realty far transcends that. As much as we could possibly grasp of that True Reality, we will always fall short in our perception due to our finite limitations[17]. His True Reality is *Ain Sof Baruch Hu* — **Infinity Itself**, and will therefore always be much, much greater than anything we, as finite beings, can ever imagine[18].

---

[14]*"Lecha dumiyah tehillah"* — "For You silence is a praise" (Tehillim 65-2). "The silence is a praise to You because your praise is limitless, and the one who is lengthy in praise, is really just detracting" (Rashi, ibid).
[15]*Sefer Da'as Tvunos, os mem-vav:* "Because He, *may His Name be blessed*, His Existence is known to us with certainty since it is logically imperative; however His Essence is not possible for us to grasp at all".
[16]*Sefer Mishnas Chasidim (Haichal Aleph, perek aleph, mishna beis):* "The Light of *Ain Sof* – Who is known [in] His Existence and not His Essence."
[17]This is stated explicitly in the *Navi* (Prophets): *"Ki lo machshevosai machshevoseichem"* — "For My Thoughts have no similarity to your thoughts" (Yeshayahu 55-8). Hashem is telling us: "Our thoughts are from two different sources; mine are Thoughts that are sourced in Infinity, while your thoughts are finite."
[18]The logical question then becomes, so how could we ever relate to Hashem at all? The holy Zohar answers (*Parshas Bo, Chelek Beis, daf mem-beis, amud beis*), that Hashem has created a "medium" by

He is beyond everything we can grasp in our finite world; and He is beyond everything in the universe which we can grasp. His Reality extends beyond the universe, and the entire universe is really located *in Him*[19]. He is the First Cause and Creator for everything in the universe that we know. He is where we come from and therefore, is the objective "starting point" of all. He is also where we're going to and is therefore, the *objective* "goal" of everything we're trying to reach as well.

Now that we have clarified what this *first axiom* is – the absolute starting point "for everything" in this world is Hashem, Whose Existence we can grasp but not His Essence – we can begin to apply it, and even to test it, in our lives. We need to see how it holds true through our own personal experience.

But beforehand, it will help us greatly to become attentive to the truth of this axiom if we just *notice* how much it actually plays a role in our everyday lives in this world.

### Chapter Quick Points

> The simple way we relate to Hashem is as "the One Who brings all that we know of into existence".

> The deeper way we relate to Hashem is as Ain Sof *Baruch Hu* – He is Infinity Itself.

> What we can grasp for sure about Hashem is that He Exists. However, His True Essence is beyond our finite grasp.

---

means of which we can come *in some way* to know Who He is, and, ultimately, to develop a Real relationship with Him. The use of this medium is contingent, however, upon our constant awareness that this medium is only a "stepping stone" in order for us to be able to grasp Hashem's Essence in some way, but has nothing to do with Hashem Himself. Hashem's True and Ultimate Essence is far beyond even the created reality of that medium.

[19] "Hakadosh Baruch Hu is the place for the world, and the world is not the place for Him" (*Bereishis Rabah*, *parsha* 68-9).

## 3

# What Everyone in the World is Really Looking For

*In This Chapter:*

> Why is everyone drawn to "worship" something greater?

> What causes a person to "worship" one entity more than another?

> What is the best "worship" to have?

If we allow ourselves the opportunity to just *imagine* accepting this first axiom as the true "starting point" – even before "testing" it – we can begin to take notice of the tremendous effect that it has upon every human being. We can see throughout our lives, that all of mankind – whether consciously or sub-consciously – are drawn to *seek Infinity* in this world.

The yearning desire *to connect to Infinity* is clearly the underlying drive within human consciousness that motivates any human being toward any goal. Whatever any person in this world decides to choose as his life's purpose, is unequivocally intertwined with the fact that man has an underlying, unexplainable pull toward the *Infinite*.

## Searching for the Infinite

You'll notice that people's goals in the world are almost always about becoming larger and greater. They may seek power, fame, or perhaps greater and more intense pleasures. Really, what they are all looking for is to connect to a level of Infinity; this is because in essence – whether they know it or not – the objective goal of their existence is to connect to *Ain Sof Baruch Hu* – the True and Ultimate Infinity.

Mankind is actually "hard-wired" to constantly yearn for something greater. In order to lead people to the objective goal of their existence, G-d has implanted within the human consciousness a *need* to always subordinate himself to, or to "worship", something greater.

## Worship of Something Greater

Everyone in the world worships something. For those who genuinely have a religion which consecrates G-d in their lives, man's natural drive for worship is focused toward the worship of G-d. Yet for those who don't **he may end up "worshiping" some man-made "god"** have religion, the drive to worship something doesn't just "turn off". It's often misdirected and used to worship elements that are not G-dly at all. Because the need to worship is always active in man's consciousness, he may end up "worshiping" some alternative or man-made "god" just because it satisfies this need.

For example, some people subjectively choose an altruistic value, whether "world peace", "environmental preservation", "education of the underprivileged", etc. and then they, literally, "give up their lives" to proliferate the application of that value.

When a person is willing to sacrifice his time – which is his life – and to nullify his plans, for something that is unconnected to his personal needs, he is in essence declaring: "This person/object/value is greater *than me*. It's worth nullifying *my* life [*or even part of it*], for the sake of this greater reality".

That is, in effect, "worship".

Some people worship the 'god' of money. When they are in the midst of a profitable business deal, they can't relate to anything else – no matter how important it may be. Other people worship sports. When they are watching a decisive game, they simply cannot relate to anything else. These behaviorisms are a clear sign of "worship". When all of their energies and focus become totally subjugated to another entity, they are *de facto* worshiping it.

Almost anything in the world can be worshiped. Some people choose to take on a political cause; others embrace science or a social issue. Still others choose a specific profession or art and decide "this is what I want to dedicate my life to".

Some choose less lofty goals: they may feel that they wish to dedicate large parts of their life to their dog, their car, home décor or even their stamp collection. Yet at the end of the day all of these are just different forms of worship.

**the reason a person worships anything is because he finds in it some aspect of Infinity**

Combining the two aforementioned ideas, we discover something amazing. If it is true that: 1) What everyone in the world is really looking to connect to is Infinity; and that 2) Everyone in the world "worships" something, i.e. subjects his time and energy to some entity – then we can deduce that *the reason* a person worships anything is because he finds in it *some aspect* of Infinity[20]. He

---

[20] According to traditional Jewish belief there are "extensions" of tangible and discernable Infinity which extend into the physical entities located throughout the entire world (see *Ohr Hachaim*, Shmos 19-5, piece beginning *Od Yirmoz*). [The "seeming" contradiction – of using a finite term regarding a reality in our world (e.g. "piece") together with an infinite term ("Infinity") – is really just a "paradox" (which seems only *to us* as a contradiction) and *does* have a solution.] These "parts" or "aspects" of Infinity are expressed as the natural properties or traits that are distinguishable from each individual physical entity. These natural positive attributes are the expression of life-giving force from within them which we can discern externally, and are really holistic and G-dly aspects that are revealed whenever we see/relate to/experience any given physical entity, and are sourced in the Ultimate Infinity. See also Chapter 8.

discerns some completeness or holistic nature within that specific entity, and that's why he is drawn to worship it.

It is amazing to see – even before we have verified *for ourselves* the "first axiom"– that the pursuit of connection to the Infinite has a direct effect upon each and every human being in regard to their life's goals and pursuits – whether they are aware of it or not.

## Which Worship is Best

This now leaves us with the question: "What is the 'best' worship to have?" If it is true that every human being is constantly searching to connect to Infinity and the reason that one dedicates himself to anything is because he recognizes an aspect of Infinity within it – then what makes one form or object of 'worship' better than any other? Isn't everyone just choosing to worship the 'aspect of Infinity' that *they* relate to, or that they think is best *for them*?

The answer is that every type of worship in the world will always be exactly that: only *a part* of the experience of the True and Ultimate Infinity. Since we know that every human is internally 'programmed' to yearn for a connection to the True and Ultimate Infinity, his true inner desire will only really be *satisfied* once he subjugates himself to the 'entire' All-inclusive Infinity, rather than to just a 'part' of it[21].

---

[21] Even though we cannot grasp His *Essence* on the intellectual level because it extends without limit and is beyond our capabilities to grasp within our finite intellect, on the experiential level – which works through our hearts and feelings, we *can* experience levels that 'go beyond'. Anyone who has ever experienced overwhelming love or fear knows that although words themselves are too 'weak' to convey to another person 'really' what one is feeling at that moment, the actual feeling in his heart is experienced as a level beyond and as an 'Infinite' or 'G-dly' experience. Since man is born with an underlying desire to connect to the Ultimate Infinity, he will never truly and consistently be satisfied with a 'part' of that experience but rather only when he experiences a real connection with the Ultimate All-inclusive Infinity.

Worshiping the All-inclusive Source, from which everything emanates and to which everything eventually returns – Hashem – allows for the experience of Infinity that every person's soul is really yearning for, because it includes *all* the "aspects" of Infinity that are found in the entire universe[22].

**They will never be able to ultimately satisfy the desire of the human soul**

Whereas all those other aspects, while being worshiped, will appear to seem wholesome, complete and "godly" within their limited contexts, they are really not godly at all – only "extensions" or "aspects" of the real G-d. They will therefore never be able to ultimately satisfy the desire of the human soul to reunite with the Source Infinity because they are only partial expressions of the True and Ultimate Infinity.

It is apparent just from the various life pursuits of mankind that the desire to unite with the *true starting point 'for everything'* is the major motivating factor for human beings in choosing their life's purpose.

---

### Chapter Quick Points

> Everyone in the world is constantly yearning to become bigger and greater.

> What everyone in the world is *really* looking for is to connect to a level of the Infinite.

> Every type of worship that is in the world includes some 'aspect of Infinity' in it.

> The best worship to develop is a worship of the 'entire' All-inclusive Infinity; only then will one's true desire to connect to the Infinite be fully satisfied.

---

[22] "There, by the Creator, there are *all* of the pleasures – because He is the Source of all the created" (*Kedushas Levi, Parshas* Noach, piece beginning *Od yevuar Eileh Toldos*).

**In This Chapter:**
> How can you prove to yourself without a doubt that Hashem Exists?
> What are the rules of prayer which yield detectable results?
> Why can't it just all be coincidence?

# How Can I Know for Sure that Hashem is Here?

As mentioned, before one accepts an axiom to build his life upon, it is only appropriate to verify its truth through *his own experience.*

The objective axiom that we begin with according to Jewish belief is Hashem's Existence. Hashem is really *Ain Sof Baruch Hu,* and His True Reality is All-inclusive of every aspect of good and pleasure that exists in the world. Since He is the Source for every aspect of life that exists, it follows directly that He is also All-powerful and has full control over everything that transpires in our lives.

But how can we verify this? What can prove to us beyond a doubt that He really *is* All-inclusive, All-powerful, and has full control over everything in our lives?

## A Way to Know

As we will learn[23], Hashem does not only desire our worship, He desires *to give to us* as well. It follows from this, that if we

---

[23] See Chapter 5.

choose to worship Him and then ask of Him to do something *for us*, He will oblige. After all, if, as we believe, He *is* All-powerful and He *also* desires to give to us, there must be nothing holding Him back from doing so.

So wouldn't the way for us to verify whether the *first axiom* is true, be for us to ask Him for things that we need, time and time again? Then, if He fulfills them time and time again without fail, it will become evident that He *really does* have full control over everything in our lives.

One or two times might not be enough to fully verify this for ourselves; but if we asked for many things, time and time again, and *each and every time* we'd see that our requests were fulfilled, wouldn't that be a clear enough verification for anyone that He must be present and have full control[24]?

The only problem with this 'litmus test' is that we see many people who *do* worship Hashem but are *not* always answered in their prayers; and even if they are, it is certainly not each and every time for their every request. If so, how will our asking time and time again possibly serve as a proof?!

The answer is that there are different types of prayers.

Hashem certainly listens to each and every prayer and always desires to give to us by fulfilling our requests; just that some types of prayers get answered immediately — others, only after a lapse of time[25].

---

[24] The Rambam (Introduction to *Peirush Hamishnayos* — *Zeraim*), in explaining the Torah's guideline of how to test for a true prophet, writes that this is the way to test for a true prophet as well. The nation asks of him to foretell *again and again* positive future occurrences. Only once *each and every* prediction of his comes true precisely, many, many times, does he then become accepted as a true and verified prophet.

[25] Midrash Rabbah Devorim, *parsha beis, os yud-zayin*: "Said *Rabbonan*: There is a prayer that is

The type of prayer we are referring to here as a 'test' is specifically that type which is "formatted" to be answered immediately. There are specific rules that a person must follow in order for his prayers to be answered "immediately"[26]. But once he follows those rules, he should be able to see answers to his prayers – time and time again, for each and every one. He can then know with certainty, at least *within himself and through his own experience* – the truth of the most basic axiom we have.

**There are rules that a person must follow for his prayers to be answered "immediately"**

There are three main rules, according to the teachings of our Sages, that we need to keep in mind when praying specifically for the purpose of being answered "immediately" and 'seeing' an answer to the prayer:

## Ask for Smaller Requests

**Rule One:** Ask for such results that you know you have enough merit to obtain.

Hashem has designed this world to run according to the principle of "measure for measure"[27]. Commensurate to the amount

---

answered [after] forty days... There is a prayer that is answered [after] twenty days... There is a prayer that is answered [after] three days... There is a prayer that is answered [after] one day... There is a prayer that is answered in the [same] day". See also *Midrash Shmuel* 4.

[26] Disclaimer: This **does not mean** that a person should not pray in other forms of prayer and ask Hashem for things that are appropriate to ask for which are *not* usually "answered immediately". It simply means that in order to achieve the verification we are looking for and to verify the axiomatic 'starting point' of knowing without a doubt that Hashem exists and is All-inclusive and All-powerful, it is necessary to practice *also* praying in the "format" of prayers that are "answered immediately". In order to obtain the sought-after verification.

[27] Sotah 8b: "Miriam waited for her brother, so all of the Israelite camp waited for her". [See also Pirkei Avos 5-23: "L'fum tzara agra" – "According to the amount of difficulty [and exerted effort in worship] is the amount of reward".] This principle is the medium used to define precisely the level of reward or punishment that is due to man as a result of his worship to Hashem.

of effort that one puts into his worship of Hashem, is he worthy of receiving Hashem's Benevolence.

Therefore, although a person could and should ask for all the bigger things in life — for example, that there be world peace, that there be unity between all Jews, that Hashem bring us the Final Redemption, etc. — such 'universal' requests will not help clarify whether Hashem is here and listening. The amount of merit that is necessary to achieve such results, is likely much more than we each have at the present moment, and so we will not witness any immediate answer[28].

**universal requests will not help clarify whether Hashem is here**

However, when we ask for results that we can be confident that we already *do have* enough merit for[29], e.g. for the "smaller things" that we may need *for that specific day* — 'daily' requests such as these *can* help us to clarify for ourselves whether Hashem is here and listening. For example, requesting that we be able to get to work/school on time without getting stuck in traffic[30], or that we be able to stop into a bank and make a deposit without the line taking 'forever', or that the supper we are cooking come out tasty and good, etc. are

---

[28] Disclaimer: This **does not mean** that a person shouldn't generally pray in a way where he requests a "*matnas chinam*" (Hashem's Benevolence in a way that *does not subtract* from his merits at all). It simply means that for the purpose of verification he should pray for smaller requests (which seem reasonably to be within his merits to receive) rather than for larger ones, as will now be explained.
[29] It is worth reminding ourselves at this point of the words of the Ari *z"l* to his main disciple Rav Chaim Vital *z"l*: "The greatness of the soul is not dependent on the acts of the person but rather according to the specific time and generation. For *a very small act* in a generation like this, carries the [same] weight of a number of great mitzvos that were [performed] in other generations; since in these generations the cover-up [of spirituality] has gained very, very much strength [almost] to no limit, which was not so in the earlier generations" (*Sefer Hachezyonos*). That statement was made four hundred years ago. How much more so does it apply to our times! Therefore, it is safe to assume that anyone who fulfills even some *mitzvos* nowadays — but with true sincerity, has more than enough merits in order to ask of Hashem to orchestrate the events of his day in a favorable way.
[30] This is assuming that one did not leave in the last minute — which would require a *much greater amount of merit* to be on time.

"smaller requests" that are needed to be answered on the same day. The amount of merit that is necessary to access such results is not a great deal, and we can safely assume that we already have that amount of merit[31].

## Do Not Actively Expect

**Rule Two:** After completing your prayer, do not *actively wait* for it to be fulfilled.

Our Sages teach, that even in a case where a person was worthy of being answered for his prayers, the result will nonetheless not occur as long as the supplicant is focused on expecting, or actively waiting, for it to appear. Even if the petitioner's request was already **the result will not occur as long as the supplicant is expecting it** granted from on high, it *cannot* emerge into the reality of this world until the requester *is distracted* from his active anticipation of the desired outcome.

The Talmud in tractate Brachos[32] says, "Anyone who is lengthy in his prayer and examines it (i.e. he is actively awaiting that his request be fulfilled due to his lengthiness [and his exerted concentration in his prayer] – Rashi) – comes out at the end with heartache (i.e. at the end his request is not fulfilled, and it comes out that [the] expectant yearning was in vain; and it is a heartache when a person awaits actively and his desire does not come [about] – Rashi[33])".

Any prayer that one requests of Hashem and then 'looks over

---

[31] See footnote 29.
[32] 32b.
[33] Ibid, piece beginning *u'me'ayen bah*.

his shoulder', actively waiting to see it materialize — *does not* immediately come about. When a person puts added effort into his prayer, expecting that it will definitely be fulfilled due to his extra concentration, it will only result in disappointment and heartache; the redemption from one's situation of need can only materialize when one's attention *is distracted* from his initial request[34].

On a practical level, this teaches us that in order to see Hashem answer our prayers, we must make sure to *turn our attention away* from the petitioned request right after we conclude our prayers about it.

## Check Back After the Fact

**Rule Three:** Check back at the day's end to see whether you were answered.

It is very easy to forget to go back and check to see whether Hashem has actually answered, since, after all, one of the rules is that after praying we need to distract ourselves from the original request. Therefore, in order to reap the benefits of the verification we are looking for, it is necessary to make a concerted effort to go back and see whether we were answered.

A suitable time to make this accounting is at the end of the day, right before going to sleep. Start off by trying to remember what "small things" you asked for that day in your prayers[35]. Then review the events of the day in your mind, and see whether Hashem "answered" you or not.

---

[34] Sanhedrin 97a: When discussing the Final Redemption the Talmud establishes definitively: "Three [things] come when [one's] knowledge is *distracted*: Moshiach (not when one is involved in trying to know when he will come — Rashi.); a finding [of a lost or hidden object]; a scorpion (bites the person suddenly — Rashi).

[35] Or perhaps jot them down earlier in the day as you make them, and keep the paper or notebook somewhere where it won't catch your attention (so you'll be able to distract yourself during the day).

Here's the rule of what to look for during this "check-time": "Was the *core heart-request* of my prayer fulfilled or not?"

Very often Hashem *has* clearly answered our prayers – just that *we* don't see it. This is because we tend to picture in our minds that Hashem will bring about whatever we asked for in the exact manner in which *we* imagined Him to. In reality, though, very often Hashem will bring about *the result* that we needed and **we need to make a concerted effort to see whether we were answered** were praying for, but through a completely different means than how we expected it would come about[36].

For example, imagine someone who, following the first rule, asks Hashem in the morning a 'small request' to help him pay back a $200 loan which is due that day and right now he has nothing. With full belief and sincerity he asks Hashem to help him pay it back today – somehow – as it will be too overwhelming for him to face his creditor after today if he doesn't.

He then goes through the entire day following the second rule – he distracts himself from his request and not does actively expect – yet he also has full trust that somehow, by the end of the day, the $200 will suddenly appear.

But it never does show up – at least not the way he thought it would, e.g. by someone knocking on his door and presenting him with $200. But…interestingly enough, in the mail that day there was a check for $250 from his parents – as a down payment for an apartment they're planning to rent in his neighborhood when they come to visit him next month.

---

[36] The Sages have taught us "Hashem has *many messengers* [at His disposal]" (Rashi Shmos 15-32).

When reviewing the events of his day it is very easy for this supplicant to feel that he was *not* answered. After all, no money came in specifically for him, he is just as lacking now as he was in the morning.

But if he would look a bit deeper, if he would look at what he was *really* asking of Hashem in his *core heart-request* – that by the end of the day he should have enough money to pay back his creditor *so as not to be embarrassed when facing him* – then he *was* answered.

By the end of the day he had full access to the entire sum needed for him to avoid the embarrassment from his creditor [we are assuming here for the purpose of the example that these parents trust their son and give him permission to manage the money they forwarded him in any responsible way he sees fit]. For he knows that he'll be able to easily replace the money used today with other monies that are due to come in the next week, in plenty of time to make the down payment for his parents.

Therefore, when reviewing the events of the day, always keep in mind that Hashem's answer doesn't necessarily have to look the way *we* expected it to. It is very likely, that for Hashem to fulfill our requests in the direct way *we* had in mind, it would take *a lot more* merits to obtain; and therefore Hashem did it in a way that is more concealed[37]. But at the end of the day, if you had what you really needed and your *core heart-request* was fulfilled, it's correct to view it as Hashem "having answered" your initial request.

---

[37] When the salvation comes about in an open and apparent way it 'detracts' more merits; when it comes about in a concealed way it does not require as much merit. We see this from the words of the Talmud: "*Ain somchin al hanes*" (Yerushalmi Yoma, Rama Yoreh Deyah 116) – we are not permitted to rely on a miracle; and if someone *does* merit a miracle, "*menakim lo m'zchuyosav*" – it is deducted from his merits (Shabbos 32a). When the salvation comes about in an overt way, similar to a 'miracle', it detracts from one's merits in a greater way.

## Again and Again

Does all this sound theoretical and not real? Then just try it. I believe that if you follow the aforementioned rules you will be quite surprised.

The first time it "works", you may not be very moved, as it might seem to have happened simply 'by chance'; so too, the second time, or third. But keep doing it again and again, and at a certain point you'll find yourself saying, "This *can't* just be **every time I ask for something, my core request is fulfilled** by chance. It can't be that each and every time I ask for something, my core request is fulfilled; and, strangely enough, when I don't ask for what I need, it *doesn't* usually work out in the way I wanted".

You will slowly come to realize, in a deep, subconscious way, that Hashem is not only the Infinite Creator who brought everything into existence many years ago; but also that His True All-inclusive and All-powerful Reality exists and is very much an active part of our lives — even presently, in our daily mundane activities, each and every day.

---

### Chapter Quick Points

> A person can come to know for sure *through his own personal experience* that Hashem Exits.

> The rules for praying in a way that yields detectable results are: 1–Request help with *small*, daily needs; 2–Don't 'look over your shoulder' waiting for the request to materialize; 3–Check back at the end of the day as to whether your "core heart-request" was fulfilled.

> After enough times, a person will begin to sense from within himself that this cannot be coincidence.

---

"So Yisrael, did you have time to review the first chapters I left you yesterday? Are you comfortable with your understanding of the 'First Axiom'?"

"To tell you the truth, Rav, this was all pretty obvious to me before. I mean, I've always grown up knowing that Hashem is the starting point for everything and that He's All-encompassing and All-powerful. I also know from life experience, that people who don't have G-d in their life end up — consciously or subconsciously — seeking other entities to "crown" as their personal goal and achievement in life.

"What was interesting for me to discover is that there is a way for a person to clarify for themselves without a doubt that Hashem exists. You know, there's so much atheism and doubt out there today; it's a shame that more people don't know the actual rules of how to pray to Hashem in a way that yields detectable results."

"Yes. You can see from this how knowledge of the sources can make a tremendous difference in a person's life".

"Having the sources written in a handbook form is certainly a big plus for me. Anytime someone might ask me a question now regarding how we view Hashem Himself I can just take out the handbook and show it to them in the original source. But Rav, I still don't understand: How does any of this really explain the purpose of our lives in this world?"

"That's the next chapter!"

**In This Chapter:**
> What purpose did Hashem have in creating the world?
> What is life in this world ultimately supposed to bring us to?
> What do we have to do in order to fulfill our purpose?

# What's Hashem's Goal?

Now that we have verified our first axiom and we know that the objective "starting point" is Hashem, we can proceed to the next axiom.

Our *next axiom* in regard to understanding the purpose of our lives is to understand *why* Hashem, who is *Ain Sof* Baruch Hu and Infinite, would have brought this world into existence. What is *His* goal in all this?

## To "Give GOOD"

According to traditional Jewish sources, G-d created the world in order to *GIVE GOOD*[38].

The Ramchal *z"l* explains this explicitly in his *Sefer Derech Hashem*[39]:

"The Goal in creation was to bestow good from His Good, *may*

---

[38] *Sefer Eitz Chaim* (Kisvei Ha'Ari z"l), *Sha'ar Hakelalim, Perek Rishon:* "When it arose in His Will, *may his Name be blessed,* to create the world – in order to Give Good to His creations...". See source in Appendix 2.

[39] *Chelek Aleph, Perek Beis, os aleph.* See source in Appendix 3.

*His Name be blessed*, upon another being[40]."

The Ramchal explains[41] that it is the nature and essence of an intrinsically Good Being, to Give of that Good[42].

## "Becoming One"

Since Hashem is Infinite and Complete in every way, everything He does is also totally complete. Therefore, even when He Desires to 'Give Good' to the created beings, it's not enough for Him to Give just a 'nominal level' of good; rather, He Wants to Give them the most complete and *Greatest Level of Good* that is possible for them to receive.

The Ramchal continues[43]:

"...Hashem's desire is to give good to another, [but] it is not enough for Him [to] bestow [just] a little good; rather, [He desires] to bestow *the ultimate good* that is possible for the created beings to receive."

We can now ask: What is this 'ultimate' Good, and where can it be found?

Since this *Greatest Level of Good* is not something that Hashem

---

[40] *Da'as Tvunos, os yud-ches:* "What *we can grasp*\* on this matter is, that G-d, *may His Name be blessed*, is the Definitive, Ultimate Good. And yet, it is from the innate structure of the Good, to give of that Good [to others], and this is what He Wanted, *may His Name be blessed*, to create creations in order that He can Give of the Good to them, for if there is no one to receive the Good, then there is no Giving of the Good." [\* See Rav Friedlander *z"l's* note (*Iyunim* 2 on *Sefer Da'as Tvunos*), that these first few words of the Ramchal in *Da'as Tvunos* set forth the axiomatic foundation that all the explanations presented in regard to the reasons for creation of the world, are only in regard to *what we can grasp;* see footnote 42.]

[41] *138 Pischei Chochma, pesach gimel:* "Every Good, desires to Give Good."

[42] The reason given is only according *to our* understanding of reality; namely, an understanding which is within the realm of logical progression and which can be grasped by our human intellect. Hashem's Real and Ultimate reason for the creation of the world is beyond our ability to grasp. [See Rav Friedlander *z"l's* note cited in footnote 40.] See also footnote 48.

[43] *Sefer Derech Hashem, Chelek Aleph, Perek Beis, os aleph.* See source in Appendix 3.

can give "externally" to Himself – because He is the Source of All – the *Greatest Level of Good* is only found *within* Himself. It follows that *the only way* that man could receive that Greatest Level of Good is to *"become one"* with Him – so that the created beings can experience some of the same experience that G-d has (so to speak[44]) within Himself.

The Ramchal elucidates this point[45]:

> "Since only He Himself is the True Good, it would not be enough [for Him] to satisfy His Good Desire until He can give pleasure to another [in the form] of the same good that is [present] within Himself intrinsically, for that is [Really] the Complete and True Good.

**Hashem Wants to give the most complete and Greatest Level of Good**

> This Ultimate Good is not found anywhere except within Him. Therefore, Hashem's Wisdom decreed, that the way that this True bestowing of Good should take place, will be through the opportunity that He will give to the creations to cleave to Him *may His Name be blessed*, to the [fullest] extent that is possible for them to cleave [to Him]."

He Wants us – the *created* beings – to be able to cleave to His Ultimate Reality and virtually to "become one with Him" (so to speak[46]), in order to allow us to enjoy all the pleasures that are sourced within Him. Since He Himself is Infinite, it follows that the pleasures that are sourced within Him also border on the realm of *Infinite* and are the Absolute Ultimate Levels of

---

[44] The reason we add the words *kiviyachol* —meaning, "*as if*" or "*so to speak*" whenever speaking about Hashem in regard to Hashem Himself, is because we know that our understanding does not reach the true level of His Essence and therefore everything we express is only in regard to *our understanding – as if* it were His Reality. See also footnote 48.

[45] *Sefer Derech Hashem* , Ibid (immediately following the previous quote). See source in Appendix 3.

[46] See footnote 44 above.

Pleasure which a created being can experience[47]!! It is even difficult for us to fathom such a thing.

## Review of the Axioms

To "power-point" what the Ramchal has just told us:

1. Hashem's goal of creation is nothing other than: **to Give us Good.**

2. It is not enough for Hashem to give us just a little bit of good – He wants to give us **the *Greatest Level* of Good** that is possible for us to receive.

3. Since He is the Source of Everything and the Ultimate Good, the *greatest level* of good **is found only within Him.**

4. It follows that in order for us to receive that Greatest Level of Good, it is necessary for us to become as close as possible to Him, **to become – so to speak – "one" with Him.**

**So that's Hashem's Goal: that we, the created beings, be able to receive the Greatest Level of Good from Him.** In order to do that **we must "become one" with Him.**

Just that at this point we run into a very big problem, because seemingly it is a virtual impossibility for us to "become one" with Him. As we shall see, there are certain impediments within the essence of our reality which obstruct our ability to "becoming one" with Him and to benefit from the Greatest Level of Good.

---

[47] See wording of the Ramchal in his *Sefer Mesilas Yesharim* (*Perek Aleph*): "And behold, what *Chazal* have taught us is that man was created only to take pleasure upon Hashem and to enjoy from the shine of His *Shechinah* (G-dly Presence), which is really the true delight and *the greatest pleasure of all the pleasures that can possibly exist*".

Understanding Hashem's solution to this problem will grant us an understanding of why we have to come to this world at all in order to receive the Good He Wants to Give us.

> **Chapter Quick Points**
>
> - According to traditional Jewish sources, Hashem created the world for the sole purpose of Giving us Good.
> - Hashem Wants to Give us the *Greatest* Level of Good that is possible for us to receive.
> - That Greatest Level of Good is found only within Himself.
> - Therefore, in order for us to receive from the Greatest Level of Good we must unite and "become one" with Him.

# 6

## Why This World?

**In This Chapter:**
> Why do we have to come to this world — *which is not so good?*
> What stands in our way from just "becoming one" with Hashem?
> How can we get past the obstacles?

The question now becomes, so why can't Hashem just give us all the Good without us having to come to this world?

If, as we believe, Hashem can do anything, why does He "need" *this world* as part of the plan in order to give us His Greatest Level of Good? Why can't He just give us the Greatest Level of Good without our having to come to this world — *which is clearly not so good?*

**we "become one with Him" by becoming "like Him"**

The answer is based on what we have learned already, that in order to receive the Greatest Level of Good, it is necessary for us to "become one with Hashem", and this is only accomplished by becoming "like Him".

Yet there are two things related to our essence as created beings, that make it a logical impossibility[48] for us to actually "become

---

[48] The obvious question becomes, why would a "logical impossibility" be an impediment for Hashem to be able to create a way for the created beings to receive from His Good — despite the "impossibilities"? Isn't Hashem Infinite, and so couldn't He have created an Infinite number of possibilities that could provide the desired result, even if they would be illogical to our understanding? See footnote 40 above, where it is sourced that all of the reasons we learn about in regard to creation, are the reasons that *we* are given according to *our understanding*. All the reasons that we are given

one" with Him – and in order to remove those impediments, we must come to this world to "do something" for Hashem.

## Character Similarity

The first of these impediments is that the only way for any two entities to truly "become one" on a spiritual level is by having similar internal characteristics[49] and there is one specific characteristic that we will seemingly never be able to have like Hashem.

When we describe "becoming one" and close with Hashem on the spiritual plane, we cannot use physical proximity to determine distance or closeness, because the concepts of physical closeness and distance are nonexistent. The measure of closeness or distance among spiritual existences is the similarity, or lack thereof, of their intrinsic properties: the more similar they are, the 'closer' they are; conversely, the greater the divergence of their internal traits, the greater the spiritual "distance" between them[50].

In light of this, we can easily discern that there is one distinguishing factor that will always cause us to be – not only a little

---

for our understanding are still not the Ultimate Reason as to why Hashem did what He did (but because we are finite and Hashem Knows we cannot understand more, *He does not expect from us to understand more* than we do – our worship of Him is considered complete if we just follow all the reasons that *we* can understand) . Since it is not possible for us to understand the Thoughts of Hashem, we must focus only upon trying to understand those reasons that are within *our ability to understand* and the realm of *our grasp*. Therefore, the answers that are given for our understanding *must be logical possibilities*.

[49] In the spiritual dimension, when two entities have identical properties, they merge and become one. This rule has some expression even in the physical world as well: We see that whenever two substances have identical molecular composition, they unite to become totally one when they are joined in physical proximity. Example: Two drops of water or two drops of liquid mercury that are spilled on the ground (e.g. if a mercury thermometer breaks), when joined together, unite to become one total unified reality, even upon the slightest touch of one to the other.

[50] *Peirush Hasulam L'sefer Hazohar (Psicha L'chochmas Hakaballah, os yud-gimel)*: "You can deduce regarding [all] spiritual realities: that all the concepts of distance and proximity and unity and oneness that are discerned amongst them, are only quantifications of divergent *internal character*; that according to the degree of difference in character they are separate one from another, and according to the degree of similarity in character they are joined one to another."

distant, but — as distant 'as could possibly be' from the Creator. Since Hashem is 'the Creator' and we are "the created" — He will always be *'giving'* to us and we will always be *'receiving'* from Him. In this regard, we are diametric opposites[51].

Thus, no matter how much we strive to "become one" with Hashem by aligning all of our other internal characteristics (such as truthfulness, love, etc.) with His, we will always remain 'distant' and separate from Him spiritually because of the intrinsic difference in character that stems from our being created and always *"receiving"* and Him being the Creator and always *"giving"*.

This presents a serious impediment to achieving Hashem's Ultimate Goal in creation — that man "become one" with Him in order to receive *the Greatest Level of Good* that He wants to give him.

## Bread of Embarrassment

A second impediment that makes it logically "impossible" for us to receive the Greatest Level of Good without our souls coming to this world, is *the sense of embarrassment* that the *neshamah* (soul) feels when it only receives[52].

---

[51] *Peirush Hasulam*, Ibid: "And with this, you can understand that although the desire *'to receive'* is an essential quality of a created-being (since that itself (i.e. 'receiving') is the entire aspect of 'a created-being' that is within him, and it is the appropriate [and necessary] factor to allow for and to receive the goal that is intended for in creation), nonetheless, by means of this [characteristic itself], the created being becomes completely separate from the Creator, because there is a difference of internal character to the point of his being diametrically opposite to the Creator. For the Creator is entirely [of the internal quality] *'to give'*, and there is nothing in Him from the aspect of *'receiving'* at all (*chas v'shalom*); and him, [the created-being,] is entirely [of the internal quality] *'to receive'*, and there is nothing in him from the aspect of *'giving'* at all. It is therefore clear, that you do not have a difference of internal character more distant than this, and therefore we find definitively, that this difference in the internal characteristics will separate him (the created-being) from the Creator." See source in Appendix 4.

[52] This reason was told to the Beis Yoseph *z"l* by his Maggid (heavenly teacher), and is quoted in his *Sefer Maggid Meisharim, Parshas Bereishis, Ohr L'Yom HaShabbos, Yud-Daled L'Teves* (see next footnote). The Ramchal also uses *this* reason in explaining the reason for creation of the world: In *Da'as*

**36** *It's all for the Good*

According to what we have passed down from traditional Jewish sources, even before the soul comes to this world, it was already experiencing Hashem's Good and Giving Benevolence; just that it couldn't really enjoy that Benevolence because it was overcome with *a sense of embarrassment*[53]. This is termed in the sources as "*Nahamah D'kisufah*" — the embarrassment of 'eating bread' without having to do any work for it. 'Eating bread', is the most basic example of physical sustenance and is a metaphor[54] for the experience of the souls having received the full satisfaction for all their needs from Hashem — which is itself the most basic level of all-inclusive "pleasure" — without having had to do any work for that level of satisfaction.

Since the soul had never done anything for the Creator, everything that was experienced was in the form of a gift, making the soul feel tremendously dependent and embarrassed[55] and thus detracting from its experience of the Good.

**the soul is overcome with embarrassment**

---

*Tvunos* (*ois yud-ches*) he quotes a *Yerushalmi* (*Orlah*, 3-1): "One who eats from that which is not his, is embarrassed to look at his [benefactor's] face". The embarrassment itself would create a "block" in our ability to receive the complete Good that Hashem Desires to give us.

[53] "The *neshamos*, until they come to this world, can be compared to someone who eats the bread of the King without [having to] work [for it]. The *neshamos* [in that state] are embarrassed to eat bread of the King without [having to do] any work [for it], and therefore desire to come to this world... In order to remove this [initial] embarrassment, it is necessary [for them] to come into this world and to be involved in Torah and *mitzvos* [thereby 'earning' their reward]... and then they will [be able afterward to] eat bread without embarrassment" (*Sefer Maggid Meisharim*, Ibid). See source in Appendix 5.

[54] We find in the Torah that the term "bread" is used as a figurative reference for the satisfaction of all one's basic needs (see Rashi on *Vayikra* 21-21, and on *Bereishis* 39-6). It follows that the term used by the Maggid to the Beis Yosef — "can be compared to someone who eats the bread of the King" — is a reference to the souls having already received the fill for all their needs in the most kingly and royal manner, even before coming to this world.

[55] It is not a pleasant feeling to be pitied and to be given to by someone else without having any ability to repay the giving. The uncomfortable feeling of just taking and "filling oneself" (metaphorically referred to as "eating") only for the sake of oneself — constantly, ends up taking away from the enjoyment of the experience [e.g. enjoying the eating] to such an extent, that the uncomfortable feeling of the embarrassment will very often outweigh the entire benefit of having his needs satisfied (e.g. having his hunger satisfied). In such a situation a person may very well opt to *not to be satisfied* and not "to eat" at all, rather than to undergo the discomfort. [See also next footnote.]

This embarrassment is somewhat similar to the feeling of a rich man who became poor, and suddenly finds himself forced to accept handouts from others. Because of his uplifted sense of self respect, he feels that he'd rather take nothing from others and die of hunger than to continue to feel more and more like a 'charity case' each time someone gives to him[56]. So too, the souls have a naturally uplifted "sense of self-respect" because they are 'part of' Hashem[57]; yet when they are granted individual existence and a willful sense of independence and then they solely receive, they feel overwhelmingly dependent and embarrassed.

Being in a situation where we are *only receivers* would cause us to feel so much embarrassment that it would block us from being able to fully receive the Good that Hashem has intended to Give us[58]. So much so, that we might not even be able to receive and experience any sense of good at all[59].

---

[56] It is hard for us to relate to this feeling nowadays, because in our times, unfortunately, many people are lacking the fill for many of their most basic needs; therefore, for many people very often the "greatest level of good" imaginable is just to have all of their basic needs filled in the greatest way. Because of this, many seek today to find fill for their basic needs in the forms of money, love, status, etc., and even if a seeking "recipient" were to become dependent on a "giver", it is often mistakenly construed as being good – because at the end of the day, the "receiver" has his needs filled. But our *true* natures are really such, that if we could somehow imagine ourselves receiving *everything* we needed, in a way which was *constant and ongoing* "forever", we would start to feel so overwhelmingly unproductive, that we would actually begin to sense no satisfaction at all. The overwhelming sense of constantly just being a non-interactive recipient would "gnaw" at us until it would deter us totally from experiencing the satisfactory feelings that we could feel when we have all of our needs totally met. At that point, the *more* that a person continues to receive would likely cause him to feel more and more like a misfortune and almost a sense of suffering rather than a sense of satisfaction – until the point where it would become questionable as to whether he was actually receiving any good at all.

[57] See the wording of *Sefer Tanya* (*Perek Beis*) in defining the essence of the *neshamah* (soul): "*Chelek* (= a piece) *Eloka mima'al mamash* (of Hashem's True, Infinite Reality)". [This "seeming" contradiction – of using a finite term regarding our reality in this world (e.g. "piece") together with an infinite term (e.g. *Eloka mima'al*) – is really just a "paradox" (which seems only *to us* as a contradiction) and *does* have a solution.]

[58] Note that whereas the first impediment is a "block" toward "becoming one with Hashem" (which relates to point four of the "power points" in the previous chapter), the second impediment is a "block" to actually receiving the Good (which relates to point three of the "power points" in the previous chapter).

[59] See footnote 56.

In order to solve the above two issues and give us the opportunity to 'deserve' the good we'll receive by "doing something" for Him, and, more specifically, **in order to give us the opportunity to become "GIVERS"** – Hashem created this world. He created a reality whereby we would actually be able to "give something" to Him by fulfilling something that He requests of us.

## Hashem Becomes a "Receiver"

To solve these issues and to remove the impediments, Hashem created this *world*.

The Hebrew word for "world" is "*olam*", which implies concealment[60]. This "world" is a place of "cover-up", a place where Hashem's All-inclusive Presence is "hidden".

That Hashem even created such a place as this, physical "world" is atypical. On all other levels of spiritual existence preceding the creation of this world, it was overtly clear that Hashem's All-inclusive Reality is the Source for all creation; it was evident that His Presence permeates everywhere. This world is unique in that was created – to be *different* from all

**in this world it is possible to hide the fact that Hashem's Presence is really everywhere**

the spiritual levels above it – to be a place where it is actually "possible", at least on the perceptible level, to *hide* the fact that Hashem's Presence is really everywhere.

Hashem then says to our souls: "I have created a place, a "world"

---

[60] The Hebrew word for "world" is "*olam*", which is derived from the etymological root letters *ayin, lamed, mem,* which mean "to hide". Rashi in Koheles (3-11) writes: "[The Hebrew word for] 'the world' is written here 'missing' [the letter *vav*] – to indicate that it (the word 'world') has the connotation of 'hidden'."

and a 'reality' where My Presence is hidden. And now I want you to do something *for Me:*"

## What We Need to "Give"

"Take leave of the place where you are presently (before coming to this world), and 'go down' to this "covered-up place" that I have created — a place where the beings don't really 'see' Me. Once you are there, I want **you to be the one** to *reveal* My Presence — so that everyone will clearly see that My Presence is *even* there, even in the *one place* where My Presence is seemingly concealed."

**we are also giving to the Creator**

By doing this 'task' *for Him*, we then become "givers". **We reveal His Presence initially** *to ourselves* **in our hearts, and following that** *to the external world* **around us.** We can reveal *through our actions* what we know *in our hearts* to be true, that His tangible Presence really permeates everywhere in the world[61] — even though on the perceptible level it *seems* hidden. We now become similar to Hashem even in that one characteristic in which we were initially opposite. Now, it is not only the Creator who is *giving* to us and we are *receiving* from Him, but we are *also* giving to the Creator and He is "*receiving*" from us.

This solves the issue of the two impediments and allows us to fully "become one with Him" on the spiritual plane. Now *all*

---

[61] This goal is quoted by Yeshayahu *Hanavi* in his prophetic description of how the world will look in the future reality of *tikun* (the corrected state): *"Ki mal'ah ha'aretz deyah es Hashem, k'mayim layam mechasim"* — "for the land will be filled with the knowledge of Hashem like [the] water [that] covers the sea" (*Perek* 11-9). Just like a person who submerges himself under water is totally surrounded by it from all sides, so too the knowledge of Hashem's Reality and His Existence in the world will "surround" all the beings in the future from all sides. Similar to the water surrounding a person (who is submerged in it) which creates an *undeniable* reality, so too in the future, the reality of Hashem's Existence and Presence in the world will be so tangible, that it will be undeniable.

of our internal characteristics can be similar to His – we are also "givers" and we also do not feel a sense of embarrassment when receiving the Good because we 'did something' for Hashem to 'earn' it; we are now truly ready to *"become one"* with Him and thus benefit from that Greatest Level of Good that He has within Himself.

That is *why this world is needed*: only once our souls come to this world can Hashem's Ultimate goal for creation – to *Give Good* to the created beings – now be achieved.

---

### Chapter Quick Points

> In order to unite with Hashem we must become *"givers"*.

> In order not to feel overwhelming embarrassment from everything that Hashem Gives us 'for free', we must have the opportunity to do something "for Him".

> What we do for Hashem in this world is: 1) to reveal to ourselves, and – 2) afterwards, to the whole world – that Hashem's Presence permeates everywhere, even though it seems hidden.

> Only once we reveal this for Hashem can we truly "become one" with Him.

"So Yisrael, we've just learned and seen the sources for many of the most basic axioms in the life of every Jew. How do you feel?"

**"Amazing. It feels so much clearer now."**

"Do you know what this 'set of axioms' means for us — on the practical level?" I ask Yisrael.

**"Not really." He shakes his head.**

"It means that we're here to work, to 'do something' in life."

**"Of course we are. I've worked hard for everything I have," he says.**

"I understand. You're special. But unfortunately, that's so opposite to what most people think today. Everyone is trying just to 'get out of' work — you know, waiting for the second to leave work, waiting for the weekends, waiting for vacation, retirement etc. No one is really waiting to 'go to' work, and is certainly not expecting that there's some type of work to be done once they get home."

**"Rav, you're right. You don't know how hard it is for me to find a decent employee — even for a good wage. I suppose you're saying it's the same in spiritual things — we have a job to do, but people would rather look the other way."**

"Unfortunately, yes. But whether people choose to see it or not, the reality remains the same: we can't change Hashem's plan for us. We can only change whether we choose to understand it or not."

**"Very true. So the smart thing is to face reality and focus on doing that spiritual 'task', doing that 'something' for Him, right?"**

"Exactly."

"I'm all for it…but, if what we're supposed to do is to reveal Hashem's Presence so that the entire world knows clearly and without a doubt that He really is here, couldn't He just do that Himself?

"Of course He can – but He doesn't want to – precisely because He wants us to do it."

Yisrael frowned. "Okay, but still, if He can do it Himself, then He doesn't really need us, right? And if so, why should we receive 'reward' for doing it for Him, when He never really 'needed' us in the first place?"

"Yisrael," I say, "you can surely understand this very well yourself. Imagine the owner of a company who could do the job of the CEO himself if he wanted to, yet decides to hire someone else; you can certainly understand that he needs to compensate the employee for doing the job. Even though the owner could have done it himself, since he chose to hire a CEO to do it, he then owes the hired CEO the appropriate compensation."

"Okay, that makes sense. So Hashem 'hires' us for the job, sends us down here with a mission, and – even though He could do the whole thing Himself if He Wanted to, nonetheless – since we do something for Him, we deserve the credit."

"Now I think you've 'got it'."

"But Rav, I must be honest with you and please don't be upset with me for saying it like this, but, if I understand correctly, all this Good that Hashem Wants to Give us that we're supposed to get, is all dependent on us "becoming one" with Him. How is it possible that we "become one" with Hashem? Does that mean that we ourselves actually 'become Hashem'?

"No, of course it doesn't. But in order to understand how exactly we "become one", we're going to have learn another axiom. Our little 'handbook of axioms' isn't finished just yet!"

# How Can A Human Being "Become One" with Hashem?

**In This Chapter:**
> What exactly does it mean to "become one" with Hashem?
> Does Hashem really care about us?
> What *type* of relationship are we supposed to have with Hashem?

We have learned that in order for the Ultimate goal of creation to take place it is necessary that we "become one" with Hashem. The only way to receive the Greatest level of Good which Hashem Wants to Give us is to "become one" with Him.

According to traditional Jewish sources, the way Hashem has established that we "become one with Him" is through us building a close, almost intimate, *relationship* with Him[62].

## Building A Relationship

We don't actually 'merge' to "become Hashem", but rather, *while still remaining separate created beings*, we are granted the unique opportunity to "become one with Him" through sharing *a mutual relationship* – very much like two people who build *a unified relationship* between them.

Just as two people build a relationship where, although they are in essence two separate individuals, they can learn about each other and give to each other to such an extent where each one's main

---

[62] Bava Basra 99a, and Rashbam, piece beginning "*kan*".

desire is to fill the other's needs — so too has Hashem given man the opportunity to build that type of relationship with Him.

Obviously, such a closeness does not does not start off immediately on that level , rather it builds over time. Initially the two parties are just introduced to the idea of the potential connection. They then continue to interact again and again over time, where one gives to the other, and the other gives to the one. Eventually their relationship can grow to such a point where each one 'receives' such satisfaction in "giving" to the other, that they 'receive' more from their "giving" even more than their actual receiving[63].

> **Hashem has given man the opportunity to build a mutual relationship with Him**

Building such a **relationship** — in addition to aligning all of our other internal characteristics (such as truthfulness, love, etc.), and becoming "a *giver*" — is the way we "become one" with Hashem.

## Our 'Task' is also for the Purpose of Relationship

The 'task' that Hashem has requested of us to do for Him so that we can become "givers" — to reveal through our actions that His tangible Presence really permeates everywhere in the world — also involves our "giving" to Him in the form of a relationship. Since we know that the way we "become one" with Him is by building a mutual and unified relationship, it cannot be that we perform the 'assigned task' simply as "workers" or "laborers" with the goal being just to technically fulfill what He has requested. Rather, as we fulfill what He has requested of us to do in this world, we are actually in the midst of also *building a relationship* in the very time that we fulfill the task.

---

[63] See *Sefer Kedushas Levi, Parshas Ekev*, piece beginning *v'hayah ekev*.

This is truly astonishing, though, almost unbelievable, to proffer such ideas in regard to the Creator of the world. Generally, when we, as human beings, imagine ourselves "doing something" for the Creator of All, we imagine it as being similar to a "lofty King" who is willing to accept an act of servitude from his lowly laborer. There is no idea of any *personal connection* between the King and the laborer, and we don't really imagine the "King of the entire world" as "needing" what we, the "task-fillers", do for him.

**There is no way logically that an Infinite Being would need anything from us**

All this applies all the more so, when we consider that the Creator of the world is really Infinite. There is no way logically that we could ever imagine that an Infinite Being would ever need or desire *anything* from us, His *created* subjects. Therefore, when we say that Hashem "allows us" to do a service for Him — to proliferate the tangible sense of His Presence in the world — it is almost as if He is "doing *us* a favor".

Yet Hashem has done the unfathomable: It is an axiom of our belief that Hashem has structured our service for Him in a way that we can build and ultimately experience a "mutual" relationship with Him. He actually considers our work of 'benefit' to Him, and as if we did something for Him that He needed.[64]

This basic outlook of viewing ourselves as human beings involved in building a "mutual relationship" with the Creator of the world,

---

[64] This idea, to view our service to Hashem as if He really needs and desires it, is a major foundation of Jewish belief and is termed in Hebrew "*Ha'Avodah Tzorech Gavohah*". In regard to this truism the *Shela Hakadosh* (*Sha'ar Hagadol*, piece beginning *v'davar zeh*) writes: "'The concept... that the *Avodah* (our service of Hashem) is a **need** for the [One] Above — is explicit in the written Torah.... reiterated in the *Neviim*, and emphasized a third time in the *Kesuvim*. It is [also found] in the *Mishnah*, the Talmud, the *Midrashim*...and the *Zohar*'. [Some of these sources include: Devorim 33-26, Brachos 7a, Midrash Eicha Rabasi 1-6, Zohar Chelek 3, 4-2.] Although in regard to a spiritual perspective beyond our present reality, our actions are considered as not making a difference in regard to the Infinite Reality of Hashem (see Iyov 35-7), within the context of our reality in this world, we are expected to believe that our *Avodah* **really does** make a difference to Hashem.

is one of the major distinctions between Judaism and all other religions of the world. In other religions, the idea of "god" does not automatically include that he have a "good relationship" with all his creations. There are concepts of "superiority" and "subjugation", of "benevolence" and "judgment" – but all within the context of "him" being much, much greater than his subjects. There is never the idea at all of the subjects, the creations, having a "close relationship with him" and certainly not being able **to benefit him**[65].

Although the Creator is Infinite and the created beings are finite – and that, by definition, makes us "infinitely" more insignificant than He – nonetheless, it is specifically a traditional Jewish belief that the Creator Wills to have an "equal" and mutual relationship with us. He is in Essence, Good, and He wants to Give of that Good to those He created – as much as they could possibly receive of it – from the same Greatest Level of Good – that He has within Himself.

## A Two-way Relationship

Hashem has even given us the ability to experience a two-way (so to speak[66]) give-and-take relationship with Him. From our side, we "give Him" what He "needs" and what He has requested that we do: fulfill His commandments[67] in a way that reveals

---

[65] It is only natural for people, when left to their own perceptions, to picture things in a way where there is *no* mutual relationship between the Creator and the created; because, from a human perspective, to say that created beings should be related to as "equals" to their Creator, is counterintuitive – all the more so if we accept and believe that The Creator's Reality is really without any limit. We, in the belief system of Judaism, nonetheless accept this as axiomatic as we are told in the Torah by the Creator Himself (Vayikra, 26-12): "V'hishalachti b'sochachem", and Rashi explains from Chazal: "Atayel emachem b'Gan Eden" – "I will walk [together] with you in Gan Eden".

[66] See footnote 44.

[67] This is the simple translation for the Hebrew word: *mitzvos* – the actions which Hashem has instructed us to perform. However, the *Sefer Ma'or Eynaim* (Parshas B'ha'aloschah, piece beginning v'yidaber) points out, that the word *mitzvah* itself includes within it as well the connotation of "connection" – bringing two entities *together*. According to that, the *mitzvos* are to be understood as a means to connect,

His Presence tangibly in this world; and from His side, He Gives us everything we need[68].

The Ramchal explains very clearly how the goal of building the two-way relationship extends even beyond the technical fulfillment of the commandments:

Referring to the Talmudic passage[69] — *"Fortunate is the one whose toil is in [the understanding and fulfillment of] Torah, **and** who brings nachas ruach to his Creator"*, he goes on to emphasize that our goal in the worship of Hashem is *not only* the technical fulfillment of the mitzvos — *"toil in [the understanding and fulfillment of] Torah"*; the goal beyond is **giving to the relationship** — *"who brings nachas ruach (a "sense of satisfaction") to his Creator"*.

> **a son will naturally desire to bring his father "nachas ruach"**

He compares the relationship that we build with Hashem to that of a son who truly loves his father. Such a son will naturally desire to bring his father *"nachas ruach"* (a sense of satisfaction) because *he truly desires to make his father happy,* and is not just satisfied with doing only what he "has to" for him.

He writes[70]:

*"Chazal* have said (Brachos 17a): Fortunate is the person whose toil is in Torah, *and who brings nachas ruach to his Creator.*

---

i.e. they are "connectors" to build a relationship, and not just "commands". See source in Appendix 6.
[68] See Midrash *Bamidbar Rabbah* (4-4) where this give-and-take relationship is explicitly defined: "The *nefesh* (soul) and the Torah are compared to a candle...Says *Hakadosh Baruch Hu* to man, 'My candle is in your hand, and your candle is in My Hand. My candle is in your hand — that is the Torah; your candle is in My Hand — that is the *nefesh* (soul). If you have protected My candle, I [will] protect yours; and if you extinguish My candle, I [will] extinguish yours...as [is] written: "Just be cautious to protect unto yourself [the Torah] and be very cautious to protect your *nefesh* (Devorim, 4-9)."
[69] Brachos 17a.
[70] *Sefer Mesilas Yesharim,* Perek 18, piece beginning *"Henei shoresh".* See source in Appendix 7.

And the idea is, that the *mitzvos* which are incumbent upon each Jew are well known, and their obligation is known how much is required. However, someone who truly loves the Creator, *may His Name be blessed,* a true love, will not try and exempt himself with **the son will do for his father even that which was not told to him explicitly** that which is known to be the [minimum] requirement for all of Yisrael; rather, it will occur to him what occurs to a son who [truly] loves his father.

[And that is,] that if his father will reveal his thoughts just a little bit, that he desire some specific item [or task], the son will already invest *added effort toward [acquiring] that item and in doing that task as much as he can.* And [this], even though his father did not mention the request more than one time and [even then] only hinted to it, that is already enough for the son to understand where his father's intent is heading [and he will] do for him *even that which was not told to him explicitly,* since he can judge on his own that the item [or act] will bring *nachas ruach* to him.

And behold, this is something that we see [clearly] with our eyes that comes about at all times and in every moment between any [two true] comrades and friends, between a husband and his wife and between a father and his son. The rule is: between any [two] who the love between them is truly strong, that [the one] will not say, 'I was not commanded [to do] more, it is enough for me [to do only] that which I was commanded explicitly'; rather, from what he was commanded [explicitly], he will extrapolate to the intent of the instructor, and he will try to do for him whatever he can judge that will be for him *nachas.*"

How Can A Human Being "Become One" with Hashem? **49**

**The technical fulfillment of the commands is not the ultimate goal**

We can see from the words of the Ramchal that fulfilling our 'task' for Hashem in this world is not only about doing whatever we were commanded explicitly – in order to 'earn' our 'wages' as we would from an employer; our very task is a means to build a relationship. The technical fulfillment of the commands is not the ultimate goal as much as is to extrapolate from what was commanded explicitly *what it is that Hashem desires from us* by commanding us with that act, and then to do for Him even those things *that He did not command for explicitly* – in addition to precisely fulfilling all of those things which were commanded explicitly – in order to give Him *nachas* and make *Him* happy.

## The Relationship Continues to Build

Even beyond the level of "giving" *nachas*, the relationship we share with Hashem can continue to grow onward to the highest level of closeness known to us in this world, when the relationship progresses from sincere care and even sacrifice, on to the level of intimate.

The relationship between Hashem and the Jewish souls is not only like that of a father to a son, but even like that of a man to the wife of his youth, who's entire longing is for each other[71].

We also see how *Chazal* in the *Gemara* and *Midrashim* consistently refer to the relationship that we build with Hashem as being similar to the closest relationship known to us, namely, the

---

[71] *Sefer* Da'as Tvunos, *os kuf-lamed*. This is the metaphoric setting of Shir Hashirim, which Chazal refer to as the "song" which is sung between a soul to his Creator at the highest level called "Kodesh Kadoshim" (*Mishna* Yadayim 3-5).

relationship between husband and wife[72], where, ideally, each one's main intent is *to give to the other.*

This is the way we "become one" with Hashem. We don't actually merge in our "becoming Hashem", but rather, *while still remaining separate created beings,* we are granted the unique ability and opportunity to "become one with Him" through achieving *a mutual and unified relationship.*

The ultimate goal in everything we do is to bring the level of relationship that we have with the Creator to higher and higher levels. The more that we extend ourselves for Hashem within the relationship, the more that He extends Himself (so to speak) – both in this world[73] and beyond – for us.

---

### Chapter Quick Points

> "Becoming one with Hashem" means that we develop a *mutual* relationship with Him.

> All the "work" and the mitzvos that we do for Him are really for the purpose of building the relationship.

> The Jewish goal in life which follows the fulfilling of all the mitzvos is: giving "*nachas ruach*" to Hashem.

---

[72] See Rashi on Shmos (19-17) who quotes a wording of *Chazal* that indicates the relationship between Hashem and the Jewish people as being similar to that of a *chosson* and *kallah,* and Rashi on Bava Basra (99a, piece beginning *kan b'zman*) who explains a wording of *Chazal* that indicates the relationship between Hashem and the Jewish people as being similar to that of a husband and wife.
[73] Although the main time to experience the goal of "becoming one with Hashem" is *after* we complete our task in this world, we find in the words of Chazal that a noticeable degree of that level can be already be achieved in this world as well. The blessing that the Rabbis would give their students when they would graduate the house of study and begin on their way toward their physical pursuits in life is: "You should merit experiencing your world – of future reward – *within* your lifetime – when you are still in this world (Brachos 17a, according to *Shitah Mekubetzes*). See source in Appendix 8.

"So Yisrael, how did you feel after reading the additional Chapter last night?"

"Wow, I must say that I never saw it like that, I never realized how really central the relationship that we have with Hashem is to everything that we do 'for Him'."

"Yes, I guess if we had to sum up in some way what the main objective to focus on is, it would be that we need to constantly build our relationship with Hashem throughout our lives because that is the way we "become one" with Him."

"Rav, but I have to be honest again by telling you that something is still missing for me here."

"And that is?"

"Well, according to what we learned that Hashem is Really Infinite and therefore has no form or definition whatsoever, how can we ever 'desire' a relationship with Him? We're created beings and finite, and you know as well as I do, Rav, that all of our relationships are based on experiencing something physical: you have a friend, a relative, a mentor — you 'see' them. What you are experiencing is them. But in regard to Hashem, sure, we know in general that He's the source for everything, but we can never identify any one creation as it being Him; if so, how can we ever 'experience' Him 'enough' that we should come to a level to 'desire' the relationship at all? I'm not even referring to what you call wanting 'to give Him nachas' and wanting to 'make Him happy' more than anything. Is what I'm saying making any sense?"

"It sure is, Yisrael, and you're one hundred percent correct. So let's get ready for the next chapter!"

In This Chapter:
> In the mutual relationship, how can we tangibly feel every day what Hashem gives to us?
> What should we be doing in those moments that we feel a level of "G-dly" pleasure?

8

# Feeling Hashem's 'Tangible' Reality by *Experience*[74]

Every relationship must include interaction. If the way we "become one" with Hashem is in the form of a relationship, we need some form of interaction with Him. But where is there any point of real interaction? We certainly interact with Hashem 'from our side' by performing each and every day the commandments which He has requested of us to do; but what is it that He does each and every day *for us*?

In a general way, we can know that *everything we have* is from Hashem – the First Source of 'everything'. He brought us into

---

[74] Disclaimer: The tool described in this chapter can only be properly used, in general, *after* one has already practiced at least a small amount of abstention (*prishus*). The 'enjoyment of the experience' needs to be experienced *in a balanced way* in order for it to bring to a pure feeling of connection to Hashem. During the childhood years, a person's natural conditioning can often lead to a connection with his physical experiences, such as eating, in a way that is extreme (for example, if he got used to using food as a means to compensate for a feeling of warmth that was extremely missing in his upbringing). In such a case his enjoyment of the food may be coming from a place of dependency and an urgent desire to fill a pressing emotional lack, and is not really the same as the "pure" enjoyment of the food that one feels when he has always been surrounded by a positive and satisfying environment. In order to "separate" the dependent feeling from the positive, truly enjoyable pleasure, he must first "disconnect" his "experiential self" from its conditioned manner of experiencing the food, this is done by abstaining *slightly* from extra amounts of food or extra tastiness in the food, and eating more of what will satisfy his real necessary and needed amount of food and, at the same time, include the appropriate nutritional value. After practicing abstention to the point where he *truly* no longer feels the pull toward eating which he originally felt (that was conditioned to be used as a fill for an emotional need), **then** he can properly use the tool described in this chapter. [This is true for all other physical experiences as well.]

the world, He has given us enough food to survive until today, He gave us parents, family, a home, etc. and certainly if we train ourselves to thank daily for the various facets of our life, it will help us greatly to feel more *as if Hashem is now granting to us* each one of those elements from anew each and every day. Therefore, the acknowledgement of what we have through our gratitude makes it feel *as if* what we already had yesterday is being given to us today in a real interactive way, and is a very important tool in building a relationship with Hashem.

But there is an additional tool that we can use in a more specific way that will feel like *actual* positive interaction from anew each and every day. This tool can even allow for us to develop such intense feelings of positivity for His "giving" toward us, that over time can build into a relationship of overflowing positive emotions for Him.

That tool is "*Experience*".

## What is an Experience?

According to traditional Jewish sources, a "piece" of Hashem's Infinity is hidden *within each experience*[75].

From the time of creation, Hashem has embedded 'aspects of His Infinity' within each and every physical experience in this world[76].

These Infinite, G-dly *levels of pleasure* which are spread throughout

---

[75] The *Ohr Hachaim* teaches us (Shmos 19-5): "An additional hint [in this verse] is to a lofty secret, according to what is passed down to us [through the chain of generations] that '*branches of holiness*' were spread [from the time of creation] through[out] the [entire] world." See source in Appendix 9.
[76] *Ohr Hachaim*, Ibid: "Branches of holiness are spread through[out] the [entire] world; and there is no real possibility for them to be *extracted* except through [the] Jewish people." Hashem, when giving us the Torah, gave the Jewish people an assignment: to "extract" these "branches" or "aspects of holiness" from those places where they are hidden. The way the "aspects of holiness" are "extracted" is by reconnecting the energy and feel of all those experiences found throughout the world to their Source – Hashem [as will be explained in the continuation of this chapter]. (This understanding of "extracting the aspects of holiness" I heard from my Rebbe in *hashkafah*, Rav Chaim Yaakov Goldvicht, *of blessed memory*.)

the world are termed in the Jewish holy writings as *nitzotzos* – G-dly "sparks"[77]. The reason the metaphor of a "spark" is used, is that just like a spark is an actual piece of fire, but if during its short existence it doesn't catch on to any combustible material it just fades out of tangible reality; so too the "sparks of holiness" – which are actual "pieces of Infinity" and are located in the physicality of this world – if during their short tangible existence (while in the midst of experiencing the physical pleasure) the feel of the experience doesn't "catch on" to connect to the "Source of Infinity", it just "fades out of the tangible reality" and is forgotten.

Each time that we partake of, or experience, any physical pleasure, we are in essence experiencing a 'little bit' of Hashem's Infinity. The "spark of holiness" was initially dormant in the form of the positive pleasure hidden within each physical experience, and when we partake of it and **we have the choice of connecting that experience back to its Source** "*experience*" it, we feel the aspect of G-dly pleasure that was hidden within it. At that moment, we have the choice of "connecting" that experience back to its Source – Hashem – or not to.

These types of pleasures pass in and out of our day hundreds of times. If we pay attention to them and recognize that the pleasures we are experiencing are really the 'aspects of Infinity' hidden within physicality, then we can use those experiences to 'spark' our connection with Hashem. But if we fail to make any connection between those experiences and the Source, Infinite Creator, then they flare up and are enjoyable for the moment, but quickly fade out of any type of tangible existence once they pass.

---

[77] In the *Zohar Hakadosh* and the writings of the Ari z"l (*Eitz Chaim, Sha'ar yud-ches, perek heh, m"t*) they are referred to as *nitzotzos* – "sparks". In the *Ohr Hachaim* (Shmos 19-5) they are referred to as "*branches of holiness*".

**Hashem is giving to us in a positive interactive way every day**

It is these experiences which are Hashem's way of "giving" to us in a positive interactive way each and every day. Hashem certainly wants us to partake of these experiences – the proof being that He implanted human nature with needs[78]; yet at the same time he warns us not to partake of those experiences that He has outlined which will serve only to draw us further away from Him. (The reason for physical experiences which are *prohibited* will be explained, with G-d's help, in a later chapter. The continuation of the present chapter will relate *only* to such pleasures of experience **which are permissible.**)

The fact that we eat different foods each day, see beautiful scenery, listen to enjoyable music, examine the wisdom hidden in the physical world, etc. are all examples of positive experiences that we are exposed to daily in a permissible way. When we can "connect" the fleeting pleasure to its Source, we end up strengthening our relationship with the One who we know it all comes from.

But how exactly do we "re-connect" them to their Source? What is it that we need to do while in the midst of experiencing the physical pleasure to "connect" and build our relationship with Hashem – other than just enjoying and experiencing a tiny "piece" of Infinite Pleasure?

---

[78] *"Re'aivim gam tzemei'im, nafsham bahem tis'ataf"* – "Those who are hungry and thirsty, their souls hide within them" (Tehillim 107). The simple meaning of this verse is that travelers, who have lost their way, e.g. in the dessert, become hungrier and hungrier and their soul-energy hides within themselves. The Ba'al Shem Tov (*Al HaTorah*, Parshas Yisro, *os kaf-vav*) explains this verse to hint to the "sparks of holiness". *The reason* that a person [ever] becomes hungry and thirsty, is really because there is a 'spark' of G-dly experience which is hidden within the food or drink that he must come to eat and worship Hashem with; *because of that* he becomes hungry and thirsty so that he will seek out that food or drink and actually eat it. According to this understanding, the fact that Hashem created human beings with needs, is because He *wants* us to partake of the permissible physical experiences hidden within the physical world and to use them as a means to connect to Him.

# "Connecting" is through Thinking

The "reconnecting"[79] of the "sparks" to their Source, is accomplished simply by means of "thinking"[80]. Every "spark" is really the hidden element within a physical 'housing' that awards a person a "miniature" experience of a G-dly, Infinite pleasure that really emanates from the Source. The way to "reconnect" the experience back to its Source is simply *to think about the Source while* experiencing the pleasure.

Every time that we partake of any physical experience in this world, we experience its unique "taste"[81]. The 'taste' of the experience is pleasurable[82] – even "G-dly" when you think about it[83]. At the moment that we experience the pleasant "taste", we have a very critical choice to make. The choice is whether, at that moment, we choose *to think about Hashem* or not. The choice we make each and every time that we go through such a physical experience is what can directly affect how much closer we feel in our everyday life to forming a strong and bonding relationship with Hashem.

## What to Think About

The *Meor Einayim*[84] directs us as to what we should be thinking:

"The way to worship Hashem even through the physical pleasures of this world such as eating, drinking, etc. is to think to

---

[79] In many deeper sources (*Sefer Megaleh Amukos, Parshas Vayeshev, ofan kaf*) the word used to describe this process is *"l'ha'alos"* – meaning "to extract" or "to uplift".

[80] See *Zohar Hakadosh, Parshas Pekudei*, 254; *Sefer Eitz Chaim, Sha'ar yud-ches, perek heh, m"t; Sefer Ta'amei Hamitzvos, Ekev* – that there is *"birur"* (separation and uplifting) specifically through *machshavah* (thought).

[81] *Meor Einayim* (*Parshas Matos*, piece beginning *va'yidaber*): "The main sustenance that the person is sustained from and adds to him strength is the holy 'spark' that is in that food – which is the *good taste* that the person tastes in that food or drink." See source in Appendix 10.

[82] When experienced in moderation. Extremes could cause the bitter to taste sweet and the sweet to taste bitter – see Rambam *Hilchos Deyos*, chapter 2-1.

[83] See footnote 21.

[84] *Sefer Meor Einayim, Parshas Vaeschanan*, piece beginning *v'ahavta*. See source in Appendix 11.

yourself [while you are partaking of that pleasure]: "Why do I love [the 'taste' of] this physical experience so much? It's because the pleasure that's in it is really connected to the Source of all pleasures above. If so, **how much more should I love Hashem than I love this physical experience; because He is really the Infinite Source** – not only for this pleasure, but – for *all the pleasures* that could possibly exist!!"

According to traditional Jewish sources, it is not considered negative to 'think into' and enjoy a physical permissible experience. The physical world is not something to be shunned away and distanced from; it *can* act as a 'connector' to the Creator. The only condition is that it be utilized with a mindset that includes the Creator.

A person who chooses to *think about Hashem* while experiencing physical pleasure will soon come to realize that pleasure itself is not 'a negative'; rather it is actually a tangible "extension" of our experience of Hashem. What is considered negative about any permissible pleasurable experience is when a person chooses *not to* think about Hashem during the experience; then the experience just remains 'dangling' afterwards in his experiential memory as something unconnected to Hashem. If this is his association with it, then the more he continues to experience that pleasure again and again, the more the visceral intensity of it "covers up" his perception of the Ultimate Creator who is really generating it. But if while experiencing it he thinks about Hashem, then the pleasure itself can act as a 'tool' to connect his innermost emotions and desire to the Ultimate Creator.

## The Results of Our Choices

If when we partake of a physical pleasure we choose to 'just' enjoy it – without exercising any thought of connecting it to G-d, we generally end up describing our experience with words like "I love this food, this scenery, this music, this person, etc." In truth though, what we *really* love is the "spark" and experience of Infinity that is hidden within that physicality; whatever is physical about it is only an external 'housing' [for the spiritual 'spark'] which in itself does not include anything to love about it at all[85].

Someone who does not practice "reconnecting" his deeper experiences of pleasure to their Source through his thoughts, can end up going on for days, weeks, sometimes years from one pleasure to another, and still wonder how it is possible that he feels zero interaction from Hashem toward him for so many years of his life.

On the other hand, if at the moment we partake of a physical pleasure we choose to shift our thoughts to think about how this experience is our 'window' to sensing 'a bit' of Hashem's Infinity, it turns into a very spiritually rewarding experience. One can think, "This pleasure, which I love **a physical pleasure can turn into a very spiritually rewarding experience** so much at this moment, is really just an infinitesimal part of all the pleasures that exist within the Infinite Essence of the Creator; if so, how much more should I love the Creator Himself, Who is the Source of All the pleasures!!"

## Connecting Our Deepest Emotions to Hashem

By connecting our experiences of the physical world to Hashem *again and again* throughout our lives, we inevitably come to feel actual feelings of *love and connection* to Hashem.

---

[85] The mussar writings prove this point by asking us to imagine for just one second how the food or drink looks once the spirituality is removed from it (after the digestive process), how the person looks once the soul is removed from them, etc. (*Peirush Haya'avetz L'Pirkei Avos* 6-2). Such imagery is already suggested to us by Chazal to use as a tool (*Shabbos* 152).

Let's take eating a delicious food, for example. The spiritual 'spark' that exists in food is the actual taste of that food[86]. The experience of taste is not merely a physical experience[87]; rather it is a spiritual, G-dly experience that is 'housed' within the physicality of the food. When a person partakes of the food, the heartfelt pleasure and the added strength and energy that he feels as a result[88], is really an outcome of his connecting and having experienced the G-dly aspect that was imbedded within the food.

Although at first this exercise might seem to us as trite: "*Do you really expect that I can build feelings of love, care and desire for the Creator of the world just through focusing on how much I enjoy my food?! Aren't I supposed to love the Creator a lot more than the food?!!*" Nonetheless, try it. Even though it's true that we should love the Creator a lot more than we love our food, it's still ok 'for starters' to love Him *at least as much* as the food.

In reality, the depth of this practice goes beyond that. Once you begin to realize that the food itself is not really just "food" – meaning, it's not *just* its physical casing[89] – the pleasure hidden in

---

[86] See footnote 81.

[87] Although biologists explain that the taste-buds on a person's tongue include in them nerve endings which detect the different tastes and relate them through nerve fibers to the brain where they are interpreted, there is no real explanation as to how the *brain's* deciphering of the taste awards a person with *heart*-felt pleasure. For example, the sight relayed through the optic nerve can be deciphered as information and a person can describe *what* he sees; similarly the sound relayed through the audio nerve can be deciphered as information and a person can describe *what* he hears. But any additional heart-felt pleasure that a person receives from the *experience* of one of the five senses is not explained simply by claiming that 'the brain deciphered the messages'. Remember that the brain is an organ that processes *thinking* – not *feeling*; and the heart is an organ that processes *feeling* – not *thinking*. Therefore it must be that the *heart* experience associated with a physical sense such as taste is a spiritual one – being that everyone experiences it, yet it has no physical definition.

[88] Even if a person does not connect the "spark" of the eating experience by thinking about Hashem *while* eating, it is still considered as if he has 'uplifted' or "reconnected" the spark of holiness that was originally hidden within the food if he subsequently uses the strength and the added energy that he gained from the food in order to worship and connect to Hashem afterwards through his actions. See *Meor Einayim, Parshas Emor,* quoted in Appendix 10.

[89] "*Ki lo al halechem levado yichyeh ha'adam*" – "For not on bread alone does man live" (Devorim 8-3); "*Ki al kol motzah pi Hashem yichyeh ha'adam*" – rather, it is the 'aspect of Hashem' *that is in the*

the experience of it is really a bit of "the Infinite", then you will recognize that "loving Hashem as much as you love the food" is really not a put-down at all. It really is *one and the same.*

Someone who trains himself to "connect" all[90] his positive physical experiences by thinking about Hashem during the experience, will soon find himself thinking about Hashem numerous times throughout his day. He will begin to notice how those same emotions that were **experiences can join into one massive feeling of love for Hashem** previously aroused in him throughout his day as "infinitesimal bits of emotion" from seemingly unconnected experiences, start to join together within his heart into one massive feeling of love and positivity for the One who Created *all* of the experiences.

---

### Chapter Quick Points

> "Every permissible physical experience includes within it a form of pleasure that is a "piece" of Hashem's G-dliness.

> While we experience a physical permissible pleasure we are supposed to think about the Source of that Pleasure – Hashem.

> When our deepest emotions are aroused and are focused on connecting to what we are experiencing, we can shift those feelings to love Hashem – Who includes the "taste" of this experience and so much more.

---

bread which man lives from" (Ari z"l, quoted in *Shela Hakadosh, Sha'ar Haosiyos,* 74:1).
[90] **Word of advice:** When beginning this practice, *do not* take on every physical pleasure that comes your way *every single time.* Like anything in life, taking on a new practice, even one that is emotionally rewarding, cannot last if done in an extreme fashion. The proper way to start is to *try* this exercise once a week, then once every few days, until you can build yourself up to doing it once a day; then, once you get used to it, you can use it even more times within one day. It takes long months of practice before one can use the tool all the time. Only a practice that is built with moderation and wisely *over time* will be able to be beneficial and lasting.

*"So, Yisrael, did that last chapter make things any clearer?"*

*"It sure did! Rav, this is just what I was looking for, some exercise that I could practice in an ongoing way and get better at it over time. I'm certainly not lacking — and I don't think anyone is — of permissible physical experiences which come my way every day. Knowing that each experience is really a 'window' to 'sensing' some of Hashem's Presence in this world rather than an insurmountable challenge, has already begun to change the way I look at my day. If only more people would just be aware of this outlook, we'd probably be surrounded by a lot more satisfied and exuberant individuals."*

*"Quite so. But Yisrael, let's check if you really understood how to properly use the tool just from reading the last chapter."*

**"Ok."**

*"Name a food that you like — it could be any food, but it should be one that's high on your priority list, like one of the 'top three'."*

**"Well, Rav, without getting too exposed over here, I can tell you that I'm always fighting with my craving for pizza."**

*"Ok, great. Now tell me what it is that you like so much about the pizza."*

*"Well, it's hard to describe; it's just everything together I guess. But if I have to tell you details then I guess I'd say it's the cheese — once it's melted just right; the crust, which is not unbaked but also not burnt; the tomato sauce — not too much or too little, just enough*

that you could still taste the cheese; it's gotta be hot, like right out of the oven; then you get the steam of it, the aroma; you add the mix of pizza spices and especially if you down it with carbonated ..."

"One minute, stop."

"I'm really getting carried away here, aren't I?"

"No, it's not that – just don't mix in a second food or drink. Ok, so now, based on what you've learned, what would you do the next time you order pizza?"

"So, I guess I'll make a brachah (blessing) like I always do, and then when I take that first bite and I'm chewing it, I won't think about the pizza, I'll just think about Hashem."

"What do you mean you won't think about the pizza?"

"Like is says in the chapter I read, the enjoyment of the pizza is really only a "piece of Hashem". So I won't think about the pizza, I'll just think about all the things we learned about Hashem, that He's Infinite and He's Good, and He only Wants to Give us Good..."

"No. You just missed a very crucial point. You are supposed to think about the pizza while you're eating it."

"You are? But I thought the whole point was to think about Hashem?"

"You are, but you're really supposed to think about both. Enjoy the pizza just as you're used to enjoying it up till now; consciously feel the aroma, the warmth, the combination of tastes etc. But now before you swallow think to yourself '...and this deliciousness is really just an expression of some of the Good that's within Hashem!' That's called 'connecting' the experience to its Source."

"Oh, now I get it. You're not supposed 'detach' from the experience of the physical and sort of 'hold yourself back' from getting any pleasure. You're actually supposed to feel into the pleasure, experience it fully and then think that it all really comes from Hashem."

"Exactly."

"But isn't that dangerous? I mean if you tell a person – especially a young person like me – that you're allowed to receive pleasure from a physical experience, isn't it possible that he"ll just get carried away and won't think about Hashem at all?"

"That's more likely to happen if he's a person who's not thinking at all about connecting the experience to its spiritual Source. When a person is unaware of the process of how to connect their physical experiences to Hashem, their subconscious-self will experience pleasure in any case and it will almost certainly remain unconnected to Hashem. But if a person is aware of the process of how connect their physical experiences to Hashem, engaging one's thoughts initially in the physical pleasure is no more dangerous than a person cooking who has to mix all his ingredients together. Would you say that he shouldn't start the whole process because maybe once it's all in the pan, he'll forget to put the casserole into the oven?"

"Ok, now I get it – so I do think about the pizza and I do think about Hashem and that's the connection: when I know that all these good things about the pizza and the tastes really emanate from Hashem, then I'll know 'how good Hashem is' because He includes all of these amazing 'tastes', right?"

"Precisely."

"But then, and please excuse me how I say this, that means that now my impression of Hashem is that He's 'just as good as the pizza'?

"He's at least as good as the pizza."

"What's the difference?"

"When I say that Hashem is 'as good as the pizza', it means that my whole perception of Hashem's Greatness is limited to my understanding of the greatness of my pizza. But when I say Hashem is 'at least as good as the pizza' then I leave an opening to realize that even though my experience of understanding His greatness is limited, His Real Greatness far exceeds whatever is included in my experience of the pizza."

**"But isn't that still saying that as far as I understand, my experience of Hashem is at the same level as my experience of the pizza?"**

"True, but that's still acceptable. Let me explain.

"Hashem is Infinite, and, as we learned, really includes within His Reality all of the experiences of the entire world — and more. He is the True and Ultimate Infinity, and His True Essence is beyond our grasp. We, on the other hand, are created beings, and are finite by the essence of our existence, and therefore can only grasp finite concepts and experiences. Hashem knows this, and He only expects of us to relate to Him according to our finite reality; he knows that we can't grasp Him on His level, and so He never even expects of us to relate to Him for who He Truly is.

"That's why He prepared "pieces of His Infinity" — like the texture, aroma, color, and taste of food, finite 'aspects' that we can grasp — and spread them throughout creation, in order that we should have some idea on our level of His Greatness; even though His True Greatness is far far beyond anything we could ever grasp."

Yisrael pauses for a moment, thinking.

**"So what I need to take out of the experience is that He's 'at least as good' as the experience of the pizza — with the knowledge in the back of my mind that as much as I'll ever get to appreciate and experience His Greatness, in Truth, He's Infinitely Greater!"**

"Exactly. And that's why as our 'bank of positive experiences' builds up over the course of life and overflows, we begin to realize that as many different 'tastes' that we deposit in the bank, as many good experiences, as many sensations the world over that we are able to gather throughout life, it will always be with the understanding that in Truth, Hashem is much much Greater than the total combination of all those experiences."

**"Wow! But then why should my experience of the pizza be 'worth anything' in comparison to all of that?"**

"It's only worth as much as the experience of pizza 'speaks to you', and, from what I understood at the beginning of our conversation, pizza is pretty high up there on your list of positive experiences. So it follows that as a finite being, you are going to be drawn to seek out the experience of pizza at certain times during your life anyway, whether you choose to think about Hashem or not – because it arouses good and positive feelings in you. What we accomplish by choosing to link our thoughts to Hashem during those finite experiences that we feel most attached to, is to "connect" what we're already connected to – to Hashem; that is, to realize that every aspect that we've ever connected to, is itself just an expression of that same Ultimate Source that we're trying to connect to throughout our lives."

In This Chapter:
> Why can't Hashem just "help us out" and "finish up" the job we have to do?
> Why do our actions and choices make *such* a difference?

# Can't Hashem Just "Help Us Out"?

Let's review the "set of axioms" we've learned up till now:

*Axiom One*: **Hashem is Infinite.**

*Axiom Two*: **Hashem is Good,** and only desires to give Good.

*Axiom Three*: Since He is Infinite and everything He does is Infinite, it's not enough for Him to just give us just a little bit of good – **He wants to give us the Greatest Level of Good that we could possibly receive.**

*Axiom Four*: The Greatest Level of Good is **found only within Him.**

*Axiom Five*: In order for us to receive that Greatest Level of Good, **we need to "become one" with Him.**

*Axiom Six*: Only by 'doing something' for Hashem and specifically, **by becoming a giver, can we "become one" with Him.** That's why we come to this world    to "give something" to Hashem.

*Axiom Seven*: The way we give to Hashem when we come to this world – a place where His Presence is concealed – is by first revealing to ourselves and then to everyone in the world that His Presence is here through our actions.

*Axiom Eight:* **The actions through which we reveal that Hashem is here** and the way we "become one" with Hashem[91], **is by building a close, almost intimate and mutual relationship with Him.**

The next axiom, which we will learn now, comes to answer the question of whether we can expect Hashem to "help us out" in completing our goal in this world.

## Who is 'Leading the Way'?

The fulfillment of the entire task mentioned above, is *solely dependent on man.* Although *Ain Sof* Baruch Hu is Really The All-inclusive, All-powerful Creator and Sustainer of the world, when it comes to the realm of life in *this concealed* world, Hashem expects that it be *specifically man* who be the one to build the relationship with Him and to reveal His Presence in a tangible way.

**Hashem expects that it be man who is the one to reveal His Presence**

Since man is supposed to be the one who is "giving" to Hashem, the 'job' *cannot* be accomplished By Hashem Himself. Although Hashem is All-powerful on every level, and He could very easily just as well reveal His Presence even in this world in a way which is

---

[91] The *Ramchal* (*Da'as Tvunos, os yud-daled*) emphasizes that when a person accomplishes his task in this world and earns the merit for doing so (*zchus*) that this *in itself* (i.e. the merit that he earned) is his actual reward (*sechar*). The *task* that we do in this world, namely, to reveal to everyone through our actions that Hashem's Presence is here - which we do by "building our relationship with Hashem", is really one and the same with the actual reward we receive - to "become one with Hashem". The *relationship with Hashem* that one earns throughout his life with work and toil in order to reveal to the world that Hashem's Presence is here, is really one and the same with the ultimate reward of eventually "becoming one" *in the form of a relationship* with Hashem. Therefore, with every extra bit that we advance in the building of our relationship with Hashem in this world, we simultaneously come closer to our ultimate goal of "becoming one" with Him, thus being able to receive the Infinite Levels of Pleasure that are included within Him that He Wants to Give us.

tangible to every being, were He to do so, it would defeat the entire *purpose* of the world's creation.

In order for the world's creation to reach its purpose and for man *to "give" to Hashem*, it is imperative that only **man be the one** to bring the world to its corrected state and to completeness – and *not* Hashem.

Therefore, once man was created, *he is now the one who is in "the driver's seat"* of the world. This is so axiomatic to life in this world that even Hashem 'depends on man[92]' to reveal His Presence in a tangible way and to validate the respect that is rightfully due to Him in His position in the world as its Creator and Sustainer[93].

**man is now the one who is in "the driver's seat" of the world**

## Hashem is Depending on Us

This is a difficult axiom to relate to practically. We tend to feel that Hashem can and will help us with 'our job'. We generally do not get too over-concerned about whether the task which Hashem has given us in the world will succeed or not, because we tend to feel that if we ever get into a 'bind' – whether because of our mistakes or whether because we didn't really exert ourselves fully in the first place – then we can always cry out to Hashem and just *ask Him* for help to 'finish up the job'.

---

[92] Not that Hashem is really 'dependent upon man'; just that *due to* Hashem's 'conscious decision' *not to be the one to bring this world to its completion* – in order to give man the opportunity to do so – Hashem now *so-to-speak* 'depends on man' to do so.

[93] The Gemara in *Shabbos* (89a) quotes Hashem as saying to Moshe *Rabbenu*: '*Hayah lecha l'azreini*'' – "You should have *helped* Me". Obviously, the "need" that Hashem has for our acts, is only within the realm of this 'covered-up' world where Hashem has made a decision not to be dominantly proactive, in order that *man* be the one to do something for Hashem.

But for some reason Hashem never just 'finishes up the job' for us. Yes, Hashem has saved us throughout history in order that we be able *to survive* — sometimes even through miracles that *did* show the whole world clearly that He is in charge — but never in a way where He, through His All-encompassing control of events in the world, made sure to *maintain* the cognizance of the world on the level it had reached when things were revealed — thus 'finishing up the job' that we are expected to do. His 'saving' of us has always been more of a salvation 'in the moment'; the *maintaining* and follow-through of the message from the revelation — which is the "completion of the job" that *we* are expected to do — was always *up to us* afterwards as part of *our* assignment in the world.

**Hashem has been 'begging' us to reveal to the world His Sovereignty**

In a certain way, once the creation of man transpired and man was placed in this world, Hashem has consistently been asking of us, almost 'begging' us[94], to please do Him this favor and to reveal to the world His Presence and His True Sovereignty. Since we have learned that the whole purpose for man's coming to this world is to "do something" for Hashem, it follows that man must be the one to do it.

We can now complete our "set of axioms" with the following:

*Axiom Nine:* **All of this** — verifying Hashem's Existence and then revealing His Presence to the entire world through building a close relationship with Him — **must be done by man *only*.**

---

[94] The *Shechina* (a reference to Hashem's Presence in this world) is called "*dala va'aniya*" — "weak and poor" (*Degel Machaneh Ephraim, Parshas Mishpatim*, piece beginning *od*). See also the quote in *Shelah Hakadosh* that was spoken on the night of Shavuous in the Bais Midrash of the Bais Yosef (*Maseches Shavuous, Perek Ner Mitzva*): "And if you would estimate one [part] of a thousand thousands and tens of thousands from the hurt that I am found in, there would not [ever] enter happiness in your hearts…therefore stand my sons, my companions, on your feet and *uplift* me."

Axiom Ten: **It is therefore man's** *purpose* **and free choice during his lifetime to reveal the hidden reality of this world** – by first verifying Hashem's Existence for himself and then revealing that reality to all through building his own devoted relationship with Hashem – **or to ignore the hidden reality completely.**

### Chapter Quick Points

> Man is in the "driver's seat" of this world.

> Since the whole point of man's coming to this world was in order to "do something" for Hashem, if Hashem were to conclude the job it would defeat the purpose.

> Man *must be the one to* reconnect life in this "covered-up" world back to Hashem.

# 10

## Man's Real "Free Choice" in this World – in Two Words

In This Chapter:
> How can man possibly make the *wrong* choice?
> Why does all of man's choice in this world boil down to *haughtiness* or *humility*?

Since this world is a "covered-up" place[95], it opens a door for man's greatest failure: to "cover-up" *what he himself already knows in his heart is true.*

**He can follow his heart-knowledge even though his eyes don't see Hashem**

The fact that life in this world exists in a way where the tangible Presence of Hashem is covered from the eyes of man *does not* decisively determine that man will act in the way of denial; man has the free and equal choice whether to act according to *what his eyes see* or according to *what his heart knows.* He can follow his heart's knowledge in contradiction to what his eyes see; or he can follow what his eyes see in contradiction to what his heart knows.

What takes place when man makes 'the right choice' and follows his heart-knowledge, can be termed in a sense as "intellectual honesty". Once he has come to *know in his heart* that Hashem

---

[95] See footnote 60.

Exists (assuming he has verified for himself the first axiom[96]) and is able to follow through honestly and pattern his actions to be consistent with that which his heart knows even though his eyes don't see, is really him being honest *with himself.*

However, what takes place when man makes 'the wrong choice' and follows only what his eyes see, is that he makes use of a totally new and unnatural orientation[97] that exists only for the purpose of giving man a true free choice in this world: the ability to cover-up *within himself* the truth that his heart has already come to know. He is then not being "intellectually honest" *with himself.*

## "Haughtiness" versus "Humility"

The decision to make use of this "new" (yet false) reality – the ability to act differently than one's own heart knowledge – is called **"haughtiness"** (in Hebrew: *ga'avah*). When one acts with haughtiness, he closes off the messages from his heart which remind him of the good others have done for him. He does not attribute the true and appropriate value to anyone outside himself and devalues them to a level of nothing[98]. Since his heart clearly knows that others *have* helped him in the past to get to where he is today and that others *do* have value, his actions necessitate that he **ignore** what he knows in his heart is true.

The decision that man makes to remain 'true to himself' and *not* ignore his own heart-knowledge, is called **"humility"** (in Hebrew:

---

[96] See Chapter 4.
[97] The *natural* "flow pattern" of man is that what he feels strongly in his heart becomes exposed and conveyed through his actions. We see this from the words of Chazal which are quoted by Rashi (Bamidbar 15-39) [albeit in regard to negative emotions]: "The heart desires and the body acts [out]".
[98] Unless they threaten to stop him from doing what *he* would like – and then they do register on his "radar" – since he has to figure out how to deal with anyone who denies him the ability to "take" what he wants.

Man's Real "Free Choice" in this World – in Two Words **73** *anavah*). When one acts with humility, he is 'big enough' to accept the fact that others have helped him to get to where he is and that others *do* have value, and he can therefore respect and pay tribute to them. He is able to live honestly with what he knows in his heart is true: that there is more to reality than just *taking* for himself.

Throughout each person's life, Hashem's sends clear "messages" through the events which transpire in a person's life, to help him acknowledge the true reality. These messages awaken his heart with the realization that an All-inclusive, All-powerful and Compassionate Creator really does exist. Understandably, these messages can be a source of discomfort for one who has chosen a path of haughtiness, since these messages are a contradiction to following that which he sees with his eyes. Since Hashem's tangible Presence is hidden from his eyes, man is faced with the choice of deciphering the reality either according to *what his eyes see* or according *to what his heart knows*.

**man decides whether he will act with humility and listen to the messages**

Being that the ultimate purpose of life in this world is that man himself – and only man – should make the choice of how he relates to Hashem, it is he who needs to decide whether he will choose to be *haughty* and to *ignore* the messages to his heart – which indicate the Existence of an Infinite and Compassionate Creator, or whether he will choose to act with *humility* and *listen* to the messages of his own heart.

When a person chooses to go on the path of **humility** he recognizes the importance of those outside of himself and is thus moving in the direction of **"giving"** – which is our purpose in life – thus bringing more *tikun* (fixing) and correction to the entire world. When a person chooses to go on the path of **haughtiness** and does not recognize the importance of anyone outside himself, he is thus moving in a direction of **"taking"** – the opposite of the purpose in creation – thus bringing more *kilkul* (ruining) and imbalance to the entire world.

## Being Aware of the Choice

This has been the main fulcrum choice of man throughout the generations. Now that man is "in the driver's seat" of this world, will he be a "giver" and build his heart-connection and relationship with Hashem – thus going on to "become one" with Hashem and meriting to experience all the Good? Or will he be a "taker" and ignore his heart-connection and relationship with Hashem – thus undermining the whole purpose of why his soul had come to this world in the first place.

It is very likely that most all Jewish souls would choose to be *honest with their heartfelt knowledge* – if only they would be aware in a clear way of what their choice really is. Unfortunately today, most Jewish souls don't even get to the point of their real choice, because so much has been forgotten or become confused over the course of this treacherously long exile that they are not even aware of many of the axioms they live by and what is the real challenge and choice to make in their lives.

**today, most Jewish souls don't even get to the point of their real choice**

Perhaps the major challenge facing us today is the need to clarify the purpose of our lives and the axioms we live by, so that we not end up defaulting to living a life that stems simply from a lack of knowledge as to what our goal in life is. Doing the 'job' that we have to do here, boils down to simply following through in action on what a person has already verified in his own heart, rather than ignoring his own heart's knowledge and defaulting to act according to what his eyes see.

### Chapter Quick Points

> Once a person has verified for himself that Hashem Exists, his only choice is whether to *ignore* or to *follow through* on what he has come to know.

> The ability to *ignore* the value of all those around him (including Hashem) is called *haughtiness*. Acting with haughtiness causes a person to move further in the direction of "taking" and brings imbalance to the entire world.

> The ability to *recognize* the value of those around him (including Hashem) is called *humility*. Acting with humility causes a person to move further in the direction of "giving" and brings correction to the entire world.

"Thank you so much, Rav. I don't have the adequate words to thank for your taking out the time to write down these basic axioms regarding our ultimate purpose here in the world and their sources, and now I can properly absorb and review them. But bottom-line, Rav, does knowing these axioms help me in any way practically?"

"Certainly, knowing these axioms can help tremendously even on a practical level – but that is mostly during those moments in life that challenge our core beliefs. You see, on the practical, everyday level, there are other axioms that define our "purpose in life"; I hope that the next 'project' with Hashem's help – will be to prepare an additional part to the handbook which will describe the set of 'practical axioms'.

"But the set of "foundational axioms" which we have just completed, can also direct us in a very practical way during the trying times. At those certain moments in life, when we feel as if we are challenged to our core, when everything we have been trying to build on the practical plane seems to be falling apart – those are the times we need to reach "beyond the practical realm" and draw strength from our axioms of belief regarding our ultimate purpose in this world and to act according to those truisms."

"Tell me more, Rav, how exactly does that work? Because to tell you the truth, that's sort of what I've been feeling lately – like everything I'm trying to progress with is stagnant or falls apart – and I'm not sure exactly what I should be doing."

# 11

# Applying the Axioms in a Practical Way

In This Chapter:
> How can all these concepts be applied practically?
> Can integrating these most basic Jewish axioms yield any real results in my life?

## Life – On the Waves

Life in this world is not an easy challenge. There are constant ups and downs, and when the downs "hit", they can sometimes come with such force that it feels like a massive ocean wave striking down on a frail rowboat. The challenges Hashem sends us so that we can merit the Ultimate Good are not just sinecure make-believe tests to allow us to minimally fulfill the required criteria in order to "pass" and qualify for the reward; they are real challenges.

**the challenges themselves have to be real** Since Hashem is Real, and the whole creation and goal of this world – namely, to withstand the challenges and to "do something" for Hashem with a level of selflessness that we would naturally exert for the person whom we love the most – is also very real, we can readily understand that the challenges themselves have to be real as well.

It is during those times when the challenges actually "hit", that the knowledge of the foundational axioms can best help us in a practical way. At those times in life when we feel the challenge of our situation caving in on us like a towering skyscraper about to collapse (and sometimes even the smallest everyday challenges can feel like that – totally overwhelming), are when we can make the best use of our acquired knowledge. That's when we have the choice – instead of just "weathering the stormy situation" – to "take out" our set of the "ultimate purpose" axioms and apply them in order to reclaim our sense of balance and peace of mind.

## The Tool

In those moments, hours, days, or weeks when the challenge hits, tear yourself away from the constant recurring thoughts of how awful the situation is. Try to find a calm place away from the action, where you can quietly close your eyes for a few minutes. [Obviously don't do this *in the middle* of a situation that is life threatening or at a time that requires your active and consistent attention].

Sit calmly on a chair, not leaning on anything, your feet placed straight on the floor. Close your eyes, and review the fundamental axioms in your mind and heart – consecutively – starting from the beginning.

Imagine that all that really exists is Hashem. "Picture" the backdrop of everything you can see in your mind's eye, for as far as you can see, as being the Reality of an Infinite Hashem – and imagine that a part of His Infinite Presence is now centered in front of you as well.

**imagine that all that really exists is Hashem**

Then begin to imagine how this Reality is Truly Benevolent, Good, and Caring, and desires only to give you good.

Imagine your *neshamah* (soul) standing before this Reality of Hashem's Presence, and that the Ultimate Omnipresent Being Desires nothing greater than to impart to you from His Unlimited level of Good.

Then think to yourself:

"So why can't He just do it without this challenge? If I have no problem receiving, and He has no problem giving, what's in the way?

"Ah, I remember now, it's the fact that if I were to "just receive" in the form of unearned charity, then at some point, my *neshamah* would start to feel self-loathing; I'd feel like a 'charity case'. So I have to "give", to "do" something for Hashem.

"And that's why Hashem sent my *neshamah* down to this world in the first place — so that I could withstand a challenging moment like this, and concentrate on "giving" something to Hashem, rather than on 'what I want' and 'what I think should be taking place' at this moment.

"Okay, but what does that entail? How do I now "give to Hashem" even in this trying situation?

## Three-Branched Approach for Trying Times

1. "Well, for one thing, it includes my maintaining the technical observance of the Torah through its practical applications — doing whatever Hashem's framework of *halachah* (practical Torah directives) dictates for me to do in this situation — even if it's hard — because that's what He Wants and that's "giving" — so-to-speak — to Him[99]. *"Giving to Hashem"*

---

[99] The practical application of the Torah's *mitzvos* (*halachah*) is what Hashem has guided us to do in

even when it's hard for me – show's that I'm truly "giving" and doing it for Him, and thus I become more "like Him" (*Axiom Six*).

2. "Secondly, it includes my proactively doing 'whatever is required according to the *physical reality* of the situation'. That's called *hishtadlus* (exerted *physical* effort) and is also what He wants me to do. Since what is accomplished in this world *depends on man*, I cannot wait in this situation for Hashem to 'take care of' what needs to be done. If there is something in any way that *I* could do to help the situation, then I must do it. (*Axiom Nine*).

3. "And thirdly, it includes my not losing *trust and belief* in Hashem's Ultimate and Unlimited Ability to 'extricate' me from this overwhelming situation – even within one second[100]. The purpose of everything we're here for in this world is to "become one" with Hashem in the form of *building a relationship*; let me use this very opportunity to speak to Him and to build my trust in Him" (*Axiom Eight*).[101]

**let me use this to build my trust**

Got it!

---

every situation that may arise. It is clear that whatever applies to the situation according to *halachah* is part of the 'task' that Hashem asks of us to follow in this world.

[100] "Even if a sharp sword is already placed on a person's neck [it seems that in the olden days the executioners would *first* place their sword on the convicted person's neck to 'find the place' just a second before executing], he should not despair from [praying and] eliciting *Rachamim* (Mercy) from Hashem [that could save him]" (Brachos 10a). The implication of this *Gemara* is that we are always required to believe that *anything and everything* can always turn around totally – even within one split second.

[101] All three of these are learned from Yaakov *Avinu's* preparations cited in the beginning of *Parshas Vayishlach*, all of which he put great effort into executing during one of the most trying times of his life. Say *Chazal*: He prepared himself in three ways: for giving a present (following the *halachic* parameters of the situation, Yaakov *Avinu* followed the requirement to appease someone who he had offended [*Bereishis*, 32-21; *Shulchan Aruch, Orach Chaim, siman* 606-1]); for *tefilah* (expressing his *emunah* – belief); and for waging war (*hishtadlus* – to be proactive according to what the physical reality of his situation required) (Rashi on *Bereishis*, 32-9).

Now for the 'Hows':

"How do I keep the **halachah** in a technically correct way?

Whatever I have already learned and know, I need to follow; and whatever I have a question about, I take to my Rav, a competant *halachic* authority, and follow his guidance.

"How do I take care of what's **physically called for in this situation?**

Whatever the 'average' person – who doesn't have Hashem in his life[102] – would do under these same circumstances, would be considered fitting *hishtadlus* for me to do under these circumstances as well (assuming that it is within the parameters of *halachah*).

## Personal Talk with Hashem – Belief with No Expectations

"How do I do my part in *emunah* (faith and trust)?

I say to Hashem: "G-d, this situation sure looks overwhelming. From an earthly perspective it doesn't look like I will ever be able to get out of this; it looks to me like I'm headed for an irreversible "crash". At this point, I can't even begin to imagine ever being in a positive place again. But You Hashem, You're above all this. You can do anything. And although from my point of view I don't see any way out of this, nonetheless, I *believe* in You. I have *emunah* that You are Infinite and Unbounded, that everything is directed by You, and that all You Want to do Ultimately is to

---

[102] Because a person who doesn't have Hashem in his life, relates to everything in life through the eyeglasses of cause-and-effect that are visible only on the physical plane; and that is precisely the factor for determining the *hishtadlus* that is required in any given situation: what the illusion of the situation would require to be done if the illusion were true.

Give me Good; so therefore, I have no doubt that You could **turn everything around instantly** – if You Want to. Even in this situation that I'm in now, I believe that if I were worthy[103], You could turn it completely around for the better – in no time[104]."

Now you can open your eyes.

This "exercise", although not very hard to do once you are aware of the axiomatic concepts behind it, is life-changing. It focuses us on the reason we came to the world in the first place,

**Hashem is very much an active part of our lives**

the map of what's really going on in our lives, and on gaining clarity as to why the present challenge is now taking place. Most importantly, it focuses us upon the fact that Hashem, the Infinite Creator, is very much an active part of our lives – whether we see His Ability in a revealed way or not – and that His Reality is far beyond the present illusion of what is threatening to attack us at this moment.

The "trick" is to get in touch with the non-changing truth of that Reality, even when everything around seems to be "falling apart". Talk to Him, clean your slate[105], and believe in His Ability

---

[103] This is also the appropriate time – if one feels that he is not worthy and that he needs to "straighten out his *cheshbon* (ledger)" or to "clean up his slate" between himself and Hashem from some outstanding wrongdoing – to go through the three step process of *teshuvah* (repentance) [Step 1: Feel regret for what was done. Step 2. Verbalize quietly before Hashem what was done wrong (*viduy*). Step 3. Accept upon yourself never to do the wrongdoing again]. This process, according to Jewish belief, works immediately to absolve a person from the difficult *hashgachah* (Divinely orchestrated events) that he may be experiencing [see next footnote]. Through the *teshuvah* (repentance), a person "resets" to his initial pure and sincere heart "settings", and thus "makes himself worthy" of receiving only from the Benevolence of Hashem according to the principle of *"middah k'neged middah"* (measure for measure) – see footnote 27.

[104] See *Sefer Sidduro Shel Shabbos* (*Chelek Rishon, Shoresh Hashishi, anaf beis, os vav*) who explains that the ability for any harmful people or *tzaros* (difficulties in life) to exert control over a person can only stem from the existing reality of a bad act which the person himself had previously perpetrated; once he does *teshuvah* on that initial bad act or *aveira* (Torah wrongdoing) then, by definition, the situation will turn around for good and the person *will* come out of his *tzara* (predicament).

[105] See footnote 103.

**believe in His Ability to totally turn around the illusion of your situation**

to totally turn around the illusion of your situation — without expecting any outcome[106] beyond that which you have *already* accomplished: namley, building your relationship with Hashem to an even stronger degree then it was before, by virtue of your having spoken[107] to Him just now — and **you will likely begin to experience very real results.**

---

[106] As we have learned (Chapter 4) , when one *expects* to see results because he *davened* (prayed) or because he feels he deserves it, it automatically pushes away the result from materializing — even if it was already "granted" from Above to take place. The best advice is therefore to always put one's mind into an alternative project or pastime after requesting something specific in prayer, thus *taking his mind off his request*; **only then** can the desired result come about through the *hashgachah* (Divinely orchestrated events).

[107] See the Ramchal (*Da'as Tvunos, Chelek Beis, os tes-zayin*) who writes that Hashem has orchestrated the world in such a way, that a person needs to always forward a *request* to Hashem in order to receive from His Bounty. According to the *halachah*, a request in prayer needs to be articulated — even in a whisper — and it is not sufficient to just 'think' the request (*Orach Chaim, siman* 101-2). It follows that in order for a person to be helped in his time of need out of his predicament, he must actually *speak* and verbally express his request to Hashem. Just thinking about his request alone without articulating it (although we believe that G-d is aware of all a person's thoughts) will *not* help for the result to materialize.

*"So Yisrael," I say, having completed for now the 'handbook', "I hope that I didn't disappoint you in this endeavor."*

**"Not at all!"** *he answers with a smile,* **"And in addition to all the axioms and their sources, I also learned from this whole experience that Hashem pays attention even to my brochos (blessings)."**

*"What do you mean?" I ask quizzically.*

*At the beginning I gave you a bracha that you should have the Siyata D'Shmaya (Divine assistance) to write down the most basic hashkafos in an orderly and clear way so that it be helpful for many Jewish souls. Now I see that my bracha came true: For without tremendous Siyata D'Shmaya, it would never have been possible to put together such a handbook."*

# APPENDIX:
# Hebrew Sources

## 1. Importance of beginning with the same axioms

הקדמת הרמב"ם לפירוש המשניות סדר זרעים:

**עניין זה מבואר, שכל שני אנשים בהיותם שווים בשכל ובעיון, ובידיעת**
**העקרים שיוציאו מהם הסברות, לא תיפול ביניהם מחלוקת בסברתם בשום**
**פנים,** ואם נפלה תהיה מעוטא. כמו שלא נמצא שנחלקו שמאי והלל אלא
בהלכות יחידות. וזה מפני שדעות שניהם היו קרובות זה לזה בכל מה שיוציאו
בדרך סברה. והעיקרים כמו כן, הנתונים לזה כמו העיקרים הנתונים לזה.

### Literal Translation:

This issue is clear, that any two people, being at an equal level in intel-
ligence and in [their] ability to analyze and in the knowledge of the
axioms from which the logic[al conclusions] are derived, [there] will
not fall disagreement between them in their logic at all; and if it fell,
it will be minimal. Just like we find that there are no disagreements of
[the elders] Shamai and Hillel except in singular *halachos*. And this is
because the knowledge of both was close to one another in [regard
to] all that was extracted in the way of logic; and [in regard to] the
axioms, as well, the 'givens' of one [were] similar to the axiomatic
'givens' of the other.

### Loose Translation:

Any two people, who are equal in their level of intellectual grasp and
in analytical ability and the axioms they begin with are the same, will
necessarily reach the same logical conclusions. If they do differ at all, it
will only be in a minute number of times.

## 2. Reason for creation of the world – to Give Good

ספר עץ חיים – שער הכללים – פרק ראשון:

כשעלה ברצונו יתברך שמו לברוא את העולם **כדי להיטיב לברואיו** ...

### *Literal Translation:*

When it arose in His Will, *may his Name be blessed,* to create the world – **in order to Give Good to His creations**....

### *Loose Translation:*

At the first point when it arose in Hashem's Will to create the world – the intent in creating the world was in order that Hashem should be able to Give of His Good to created beings.

## 3. The Good intended to be Given by Hashem is the *Greatest* Level of Good; the Greatest Level of Good is only found within Himself; therefore we need to "become one" with Him.

ספר דרך ה' – חלק א' פרק ב' אות א':

הנה התכלית בבריאה היה להיטיב מטובו יתברך שמו לזולתו...

ועל כן, בהיות חפצו ית' להטיב לזולתו, לא יספיק לו בהיותו מטיב קצת טוב, אלא **בהיותו מטיב תכלית הטוב שאפשר לברואים שיקבלו.** ובהיותו הוא לבדו יתברך שמו הטוב האמיתי, לא יסתפק חפצו הטוב אלא בהיותו מהנה לזולתו בטוב ההוא עצמו שהוא בו יתברך שמו מצד עצמו, שהוא הטוב השלם והאמיתי.

והנה מצד אחר, הטוב הזה **אי אפשר שימצא אלא בו. על כן גזרה חכמתו שמציאות ההטבה האמיתית הזאת יהיה במה שינתן מקום לברואים לשיתדבקו בו ית'** באותו השיעור שאפשר להם שיתדבקו. ואז נמצא שמה שמצד עצמם אי אפשר שיתוארו בשלימות כשלימותו ית', הנה מצד התדבקם בו יגיע להם באותו השיעור שאפשר ליתאר בשלימות ההוא ית' מצד היותם מתדבקים בו.

וימצאו נהנים בטובה האמיתית ההיא, בערך שאפשר להם ליהנות בה.

*Literal Translation:*

The Goal in creation was to bestow good from His Good, *may His Name be blessed,* upon another being...

And therefore, being His desire is to give good to another, it is not enough for Him in bestowing [just] a little good; rather, **[He desires] to bestow *the ultimate good* that is possible for the created beings to receive.**

And since only He Himself is the True Good, it would not be enough [for Him] to satisfy His Good Desire until He can give pleasure to another [in the form] of the same good that is [present] within Himself intrinsically, for that is [Really] the Complete and True Good.

And behold... this Ultimate Good **is not found anywhere except within Him. Therefore, Hashem's Wisdom [has] decreed, that the** way that this True bestowing of Good should take place, will be through the opportunity that He will give to the creations to cleave to Him *may His Name be blessed*, to the [fullest] extent that is possible for them to cleave [to Him]. And then it comes out, that what was [previously] not possible from their side that they be viewed as having a degree of completeness like His Completeness *may he be blessed*, from the aspect of their cleaving to Him, it will reach to them the same 'amount' that is possible to describe of that completeness due to their cleaving to Him.

And it comes out that they can benefit [from] that True Good, in the amount that is possible for them [as created beings] to benefit from it.

### Loose Translation:

Being that Hashem Desires to Give Good to the created beings, it is not enough for Him to Give just a little Good, rather He Wants to Give them from the Greatest Level of Good and Pleasure – from the very Level of Good that He has 'within Himself' – that they could possibly receive.

This Ultimate Level of Good is found only within Him.

Hashem therefore decreed that the way the created beings will receive the Good will be by cleaving to Him, by 'becoming like one' with Him, so that they can benefit from the True and Ultimate Good in the greatest amount that is possible for them – as created beings – to benefit.

# 4. Impediment 1 to "becoming one": Differing internal characteristics

ספר הזהר עם פירוש הסולם, פתיחה לחכמת הקבלה, אות יג:

**והענין הוא, כי כמו שהגשמיים נפרדים זה מזה על ידי ריחוק מקום, כן נפרדים הרוחנים זה מזה על ידי שינוי הצורה שבהם.**

ותמצא זה גם בעולם הזה, למשל ב' בני אדם הקרובים בדעתם זה לזה, הם אוהבים זה את זה, ואין ריחוק מקום פועל עליהם שיתרחקו זה מזה. ובהיפך, כשהם רחוקים זה מזה בדעותיהם, הרי הם שונאים זה את זה, וקרבת המקום לא יקרב אותם במאומה. הרי ששינוי הצורה שבדעתם מרחקם זה מזה, וקרבת הצורה שבדעתם מקרבם זה אל זה.

**ואם למשל טבעו של האחד הוא הפוך בכל בחינותיו כנגד טבעו של השני, הרי הם רחוקים זה מזה כרחוק המזרח ממערב.**

ועל דרך זה תשכיל ברוחניות: שכל הענינים של התרחקות והתקרבות וזווג ויחוד הנבחנים בהם, הם משקלים של שינוי צורה בלבד, שלפי מידת שינוי הצורה הם מתפרדים זה מזה, ולפי מידת השוואת הצורה הם מתדבקים זה בזה.

ועם זה, תבין שהגם שהרצון לקבל הוא חוק מחויב בהנברא, כי הוא כל בחינת נברא שבו, והוא הכלי הראוי לקבל המטרה שבמחשבת הבריאה, על כל זה הוא נעשה על ידי זה נפרד לגמרי מהמאציל – כי יש שינוי צורה עד למידת הפכיות בינו לבין המאציל, **כי המאציל הוא כולו להשפיע ואין בו מניצוצי קבלה אפילו משהו ח"ו, והוא, כולו לקבל ואין בו מניצוצי השפעה אף משהו. הרי אין לך הפכיות הצורה רחוקה יותר מזה, ונמצא על כן בהכרח כי הפכיות הצורה הזו מפריד אותו מהמאציל.**

## Literal Translation:

Just as physical entities are separated from one another by means of spatial distance, so too spiritual entities are [considered] separate one from another by means of differences in their intrinsic character.

You can also see this in this world. For example [when] two people have similar outlooks and ways of thinking, they feel positively inclined toward one another, and the physical distance [between them] does not create a[n internal] distance between them. Conversely, if they are divergent from each other in their outlooks, they [tend to] dislike each other, and their close [physical] proximity will not bring them internally closer at all. It is clear that differences of character and their ways of understanding distance [spiritually] one person from another, and their similarities of character and understanding make them close.

It follows that if, for example, the nature of one of the two is opposite in all respects to the nature of the second, they will be as distant from each other as polar opposites.

You can deduce regarding [all] spiritual realities: that all the concepts of distance and proximity and unity and oneness that are discerned amongst them, are only quantifications of divergent *internal character*; that according to the degree of difference in character they are separate one from another, and according to the degree of similarity in character they connect one to another.

And with this, you can understand that although the desire *'to receive'* is an essential quality of a created-being (since that itself (i.e. 'receiving') is the entire aspect of 'a created-being' that is within him, and it is the appropriate [and necessary] factor to allow for and to receive the goal that is intended for in creation), nonetheless, by means of this [characteristic itself], the created being becomes completely separate from the Creator, because there is a difference of internal character to the point of his being diametrically opposite to the Creator. For the Creator is entirely [of the internal quality] *'to give'*, and there is nothing in Him from the aspect of *'receiving'* at all (*chas v'shalom*); and him, [the created-being,] is entirely [of the internal quality] *'to receive'*, and there is nothing in him from the aspect of *'giving'* at all. It is therefore clear, that you do not have a difference of internal character more distant than this, and therefore we find definitively, that this difference in the internal characteristics will separate him (the created-being) from the Creator.

### Loose Translation:

Spiritual entities are considered separate from one another when there exists a difference in their internal characteristics. If the internal characteristics of the two are exact opposites, they are considered to be the furthest away from each other as could possibly be.

In regard to the Creator and the created beings, there exists an internal characteristic which is diametrically opposite. Since everything comes from the Creator, He is always "giving" and never "receiving". In contrast, the created beings are always "receiving", and never "giving" to Him. This causes the Creator and the created beings to be considered as distant as possible from each other.

# 5. Impediment 2 to "becoming one": 'Bread' of embarrassment

ספר מגיד מישרים פרשת בראשית, אור ליום השבת י"ד לטבת:

נשמתין עד לא אתו לעלמא, דמו למאן דאכיל נהמא דמלכא בלא פולחנא. **ומשום דא אמרו נוח לו לאדם שנברא; כלומר, דנשמתן מיכספן מגרמייהו למיכל נהמא דמלכא בלא פולחנא. ומשום הכי מתאוות למיתי לעלמא, ונוח להם להבראות כדי למיפק מההוא כיסופא** – בעי למיתי להאי עלמא למתעסק בתורה ובמצות לעבדה ולשמרה ויכלון נהמא בלא כיסופא.

## Literal Translation:

The *neshamos*, until they come to this world, can be compared to someone who eats the bread of the King without [having to] work [for it]; and because of this the Sages have said: "It is better for a person that he was created" (Eiruvin 13b). That is to say, **the *neshamos* [in that state] are embarrassed in of themselves to eat bread of the King without [having to do] any work [for it], and they therefore desire to come to this world, and it is better for them to be created in order to be extricated from this [initial] embarrassment:** They to come to this world, to be involved in Torah and *mitzvos*, to work and to guard [thereby 'earning' their reward], and [then] they will be able [afterward] to eat bread without embarrassment.

## Loose Translation:

Before a soul comes to this world it is "eating bread of the King", that is, it is receiving satisfaction and pleasure without having to do any work for it. Intrinsically this causes the souls to feel embarrassed, and they desire to come to this world [where they will be able to do work for the King]. By being involved in "working and guarding" the Torah and *mitzvos* [in this world] they earn their reward, and can then continue on [after their life in this world] to receive the satisfactions and pleasures from the King without feeling embarrassed.

## 6. The definition of the word 'mitzva' not only includes the idea of being "a command" but also of being "a connector".

מאור עינים פרשת בהעלותך, ד"ה וידבר ה':

אמרו רבותינו זכרונם לברכה (אבות פ"ד): "שכר מצוה -מצוה". רצונם לומר שהשם יתברך נתן לנו המצות כדי להדבק על ידיהם בהשי"ת. וזהו שכר מצוה הוא **מצוה** – **לשון צוותא; דהיינו, שנדבק על ידם בהשם יתברך.** ואין לך שכר גדול מזה.

*Literal Translation:*

Our Rabbis of blessed memory have said (Pirkei Avos 4-2): "The reward of a *mitzva*, is the *mitzva*." They want (mean) to say, that Hashem, *may His Name be blessed,* gave us the *mitzvos* in order to cleave by means of them to Hashem. And this is [the meaning of] "The reward of a *mitzva*, is the *mitzva* – **[the word *mitzva* itself] connotes 'togetherness'; that is [to say], that we cleave to Hashem *may His Name be blessed* through them.** And you do not have a reward greater than this.

*Loose Translation:*

When Chazal say in Pirkei Avos that the reward for doing a *mitzva* is a *mitzva*, what they meant to express was that the purpose of *mitzvos* is to act as tools which connect us to Hashem; even the word "*mitzva*" itself includes the connotation of 'togetherness' (See Brachos 6b). Therefore they used the wording: "The reward for doing a *mitzva* in this world, is the '*mitzva*', meaning, the 'togetherness' and connection to Hashem which it brings.

That connection to Hashem is itself the reward in the future for doing the *mitzvos*, because the goal of everything we are working toward is to "become one" with Hashem. And there is no greater reward than this – because Hashem is the Source for all the pleasures in the world, and therefore connecting and coming close to Him allows for us to experience the greatest reward possible.

## 7. The relationship with Hashem is supposed to develop beyond just fulfilling the required obligations.

ספר מסילת ישרים פרק יח:

אמרו חז"ל (ברכות י"ז): אשרי אדם שעמלו בתורה ועושה נחת רוח ליוצרו. והענין הוא כי הנה המצות המוטלות על כל ישראל כבר ידועות הן וחובתן ידועה עד היכן היא מגעת, אמנם **מי שאוהב את הבורא ית"ש אהבה אמתית לא ישתדל ויכוין לפטור עצמו במה שכבר מפורסם מן החובה אשר על כל ישראל בכלל, אלא יקרה לו כמו שיקרה אל בן אוהב אביו שאילו יגלה אביו את דעתו גילוי מעט שהוא חפץ בדבר מן הדברים, כבר ירבה הבן בדבר ההוא ובמעשה ההוא כל מה שיוכל.** ואף על פי שלא אמרו אביו אלא אלא פעם אחת ובחצי דיבור, הנה די לאותו הבן להבין היכן דעתו של אביו נוטה לעשות לו, גם את אשר לא אמר לו בפירוש, כיון שיוכל לדון בעצמו שיהיה הדבר ההוא נחת רוח לפניו ולא ימתין שיצווהו יותר בפירוש או שיאמר לו פעם אחרת.

והנה דבר זה אנחנו רואים אותו בעניינו שיוולד בכל עת ובכל שעה בין כל אוהב וריע, בין איש לאשתו, בין אב ובנו, כללו של דבר בין כל מי שהאהבה ביניהם עזה באמת. שלא יאמר לא נצטויתי יותר, די לי במה שנצטויתי בפירוש, אלא ממה שנצטוטה ידון על דעת המצוה וישתדל לעשות לו מה שיוכל לדון שיהיה לו לנחת. והנה כמקרה הזה יקרה למי שאוהב את בוראו ג"כ אהבה נאמנת, כי גם הוא מסוג האוהבים ותהיינה לו המצות אשר צוויים גלוי ומפורסם לגילוי דעת לבד לדעת שאל הענין ההוא נוטה רצונו וחפצו ית"ש, ואז לא יאמר די לי במה שאמור בפירוש, או אפטור עצמי במה שמוטל עלי עכ"פ, אלא אדרבא יאמר כיון שכבר מצאתי ראיתי שחפצו ית"ש נוטה לזה, יהיה לי לעינים להרבות בזה הענין ולהרחיב אותו בכל הצדדין שאוכל לדון שרצונו יתברך חפץ בו, וזהו הנקרא עושה נחת רוח ליוצרו.

*Literal Translation:*

*Chazal* have said (Brachos 17a): Fortunate is the person whose toil is in Torah, *and who brings nachas ruach to his Creator.*

And the idea is, that the *mitzvos* which are incumbent upon each Jew are well known, and their obligation is known how much is required. However, **someone who truly loves the Creator, may His**

*Name be blessed,* a true love, will not try and exempt himself with that which is known to be the [minimum] requirement for all of Yisrael; rather, it will occur to him what occurs to a son who [truly] loves his father. [And that is,] that if his father will reveal his thoughts just a little bit, that he desire some specific item [or task], the son will already invest *added effort toward [acquiring] that item and in doing that task as much as he can.* And [this,] even though his father did not mention the request more than one time and [even then] only hinted to it, that is already enough for the son to understand where his father's intent is heading [and he will] do for him *even that which was not told to him explicitly,* since he can judge on his own that the item [or act] will bring *nachas ruach* to him.

And behold, this is something that we see [clearly] with our eyes that comes about at all times and in every moment between any [two true] comrades and friends, between a husband and his wife and between a father and his son. The rule is: between any [two] who the love between them is truly strong, that [the one] will not say, 'I was not commanded [to do] more, it is enough for me [to do only] that which I was commanded explicitly'; rather, from what he was commanded [explicitly], he will extrapolate to the intent of the instructor, and he will try to do for him whatever he can judge that will be for him [the instuctor] *nachas.*

### Loose Translation:

Someone who comes to love the Creator with true love, will not try to exempt himself in his obligations and do only 'as much as is required'; rather, he will feel a *relationship* toward Hashem, similar to what a son feels who truly loves his father — and will seek to do what will bring his father the greatest satisfaction.

## 8. The reward of Olam Habah can be experienced to a certain extent already *within this* world.

תלמוד בבלי מסכת ברכות דף יז עמוד א:

כי הוו מפטרי רבנן מבי רבי אמי, ואמרי לה מבי רבי חנינא, אמרי ליה הכי: **עולמך תראה בחייך**, ואחריתך לחיי העולם הבא.

שיטה מקובצת שם:

פירוש **כאשר יגיע האדם לתכלית החכמה דומה לעולם הנשמות** שהם שכל נבדל, ומגיע לקצת עולם הנשמות – **בחייו.**

### Literal Translation:

Gemara Brachos: When the Torah students would leave from the [Torah study] house of Rabi Ami, and some say it [as being] from the [Torah study] house of Rabi Chaninah, they [the Rabbis] would say to them as follows: "**Your world you shall [merit to] see in your life;** and your conclusion [of life in this world, should lead you] to life of the World-to-Come."

Shita Mekubetzes: This means, **when a person reaches the ultimate level of wisdom – similar to the World of the *Neshamos* (Souls),** that they are [in essence] separate (=non-physical) [entities of] intellectual grasp, and he reaches the edge of the World of *Neshamos* – **in his life.**

### Loose Translation:

The blessing that the Rabbis would give their graduating students when they would leave their house of study on their way to beginning their pursuits in the physical world is: "**You should merit to experience your world – of future reward – *within* your lifetime – when you are still in this world.**"

## 9. Aspects of G-dly experience are spread throughout the world.

אור החיים שמות פרק יט פסוק ה:

עוד ירמוז סתר עליון, לפי מה שקדם לנו כי **ענפי הקדושה נתפזרו בעולם;** ואין מציאות להם להתברר זולת באמצעות ישראל – וביותר באמצעות עסק התורה שהיא כאבן השואבת ניצוציה במקום שהם.

ואותם נצוצי הקדושה גם להם יקרא סגולה, והוא אומרו והייתם קרינן ביה והייתם פירוש בה"א מלאפו"ם כי הם יהיו הוית סגולה מכל העמים אשר נפוצו שם באמצעות התורה כמאמרם ז"ל וכמו שכתבנו כמה פעמים הדברים במעשה מצרים.

ואומרו **"כי לי כל הארץ", כאן רמז שיש לו סגולה מפוזרת בכל הארץ. וזה טעם פיזור ישראל בד' רוחות העולם, לחזר אחר הסגולה שהיא אבידתם.** והנה זולת עונם של ישראל היו יכולים השגת הדבר בלא פיזור בעולם, אלא בכח עוצם תורתם היו מולכים בכל העולם ושואבים כל בחינות הקדושות מכל מקום שהם. ובאמצעות החטא תש כוחם, וצריכין לרדת שמה לברר הטוב ההוא.

*Literal Translation:*

An additional hint [in this verse] is to a lofty secret, according to what we have passed down [through the chain of generations] that '*branches of holiness*' **were spread [from the time of creation] through[out] the [entire] world;** and there is no real possibility for them to be ex-*tracted* except through [the] Jewish people – and especially through the involvement in Torah, that is like a magnetized rock which draws her sparks to the place that they are.

And those sparks of the holiness are also themselves called "seg-ulah" (i.e. a treasure), and that is the intent in Hashem's saying [in the Torah]: "And you shall be", that we can also read as "And you shall become" – meaning, [that you read it] with a *Heh* and a *Shuruk*; because they will be the 'becoming' of [the] "segulah" (treasure) from amongst all the nations that they were spread there through the medium of Torah, as they [Chachamim] z"l have said, and as we have written [about] a number of times these ideas in [regard to] the actions of Egypt.

And Hashem's saying [additionally, at the end of the verse] "for unto Me is the entire land", here was hinted that there is [un]to Him a treasure that is spread throughout the land. And this is the reason for the scattering of Jewish people in the four directions of the world, to go back after the segulah (treasure) that is what they lost. And behold, if not for the iniquities of the Jewish people they would be able to accomplish the goal without being scattered in the world, rather with the essential strength of their Torah they would be able to rule in the entire world and they would draw all the aspects of holiness from all the places that they are. [Just that] by means of the iniquities their strength has been diminished, and they [now] need to go down there to extract that [hidden] good.

### Loose Translation:

It has been revealed to us through what we have passed down, that aspects of Source holiness have been spread throughout the entire world, and they need to be "extracted" specifically by the Jewish people. When the Jewish people learn and fulfill the Torah, the spiritual power that they generate is like a magnet – that draws all the aspects of Source holiness, termed G-dly "sparks", to the place where they are (so that they can be extracted).

However, when the Jewish people lack the strength of their Torah study and its fulfillment, they need to actually go to all those places in the world that the G-dly sparks are located, so that they can extract the hidden holiness and good from those places where they are spread. This is the reason for the scattering of Jewish people (i.e. *galus*) to the four corners of the earth.

## 10. The 'Spark of G-dliness' in the food is expressed in its taste.

מאור עינים פרשת אמור, ד"ה:

הוא סוד האכילה שנחשב כקרבן, על ידי **שמקרב כל הניצוצות והחיות העליון המלובש במאכל ההוא – שהוא הטעם שטועם במאכל ההוא;** שהטעם הוא רוחני ולא ממשיי, שהוא החיות הקודש העליון המלובש תוך המאכל הגשמי ההוא. ובאכלו ממנו נשאר החיות בתוך האדם וניתוסף ונקשר בחיות ההוא – **שהוא החלק אלהי השוכן בתוכו** – ועם אותו הכח והחיות הניתוסף בו עובד את ה' ומדבר דברים בדביקות ועושה מצות בדביקות, וכ"ז על ידי הכח וחיות מן המאכל שניתוסף בו. ועל ידי שעולה ונדבק בבורא יתברך עם זה הכח יש עלייה לניצוץ הק' ההוא שהיה מלובש בגשמיות המאכל.

### Literal Translation:

This is the secret of [worshiping Hashem through] eating, that is considered like [bringing] a sacrifice, by [virtue of] **the fact that he 'brings close' all of the sparks and the Above life-force that is 'enclothed' in that food – which is the taste that he tastes in that food.** For the taste is spiritual and not tangible (physically); for it is the holy life-force from Above that is clothed within that physical food.

And when a person eats from it, the life-force (that was in the food) remains within him, and it adds [to him] and he connects with that life-force – **that is the G-dly part that rests within it (i.e. the food)** – and with that strength and life-force [energy] that was added within him, he worships Hashem and he speaks words with feelings of connection [to Hashem] and he does *mitzvos* with feelings of connection, and all this [is made possible] by means of the strength and life-force [that he received] from the food that added to him. And by means of the fact that he has risen and connected in feeling to the Creator, *may His name be blessed*, with this strength, there is an 'uplifting' to that holy spark that was [initially] 'enclothed' in the physicality of the food.

**Loose Translation:**

The spark that exists in food is the actual taste hidden within the food. Taste is not a physical experience, but rather it is a spiritual, G-dly experience that is 'housed' within the physical food.

When a person partakes of the food, the added strength and energy that he feels, is really a result of his connecting and having experienced the G-dly aspect that was resting within the food. When he subsequently uses that strength that he gained in order to worship and connect to Hashem, he causes an 'uplifting' for that spark of holiness that was originally hidden within the food.

## II. What to be thinking when partaking of a physical pleasure:

מאור עינים פרשת ואתחנן:

ואהבת את ה' אלהיך בכל לבבך וגו'. ודרשו רבותינו זכרונם לברכה (ברכות נד א)
בשני יצריך ביצר הטוב וביצר הרע. ולהבין איך אפשר לאהוב השי"ת ביצר הרע:
אבל הענין הוא שהשי"ת צוה לאהוב אותו יתברך, ואיך אפשר לאהוב דבר שלא
נודע מהותו? לכן יעצה לנו התורה: ביצר הרע. והוא, **שהשי"ת ברא בעולם משל
שממנו נוכל להבין הנמשל, דהיינו כל התענוגים שבעולם,** כמו אכילה ושתיה
ומשגל, **שיבין מפני מה אני אוהב אותו דבר, הלא הוא רק אהבה נפולה** מעולם
אהבה כנזכר אצלינו כמה פעמים; **ועל אחת כמה וכמה שיש לי לאהוב הבורא
ברוך הוא שהוא מקור כל התענוגים.**

### Literal Translation:

"And you shall love Hashem, your G-d, with *all* your heart," etc. And our Rabbis of blessed memory have extrapolated (Brachos 54a): "With both your pulls [that are in your heart] — the pull toward 'good' and the pull toward 'bad'." And [it is necessary for us] to understand how it is possible to love Hashem, *may His Name be blessed,* with the pull toward 'bad'.

However, the [explanation of this] matter is that Hashem, *may His Name be blessed,* commanded us to love Him, yet how is it possible to love something Whose Essence is unknown? Therefore the Torah has advised us, "with your pull toward 'bad'".

And this [means to say], that **Hashem,** *may His Name be blessed,* **created in the world an example from which we can understand the exemplified reality,** that is, all of the pleasures that are in this world, such as eating and drinking etc., **that he (i.e. a person) [be able to] understand [and think to himself]: "For what [reason] do I love [the pleasurable experience in] this [physical] object, isn't it just a 'fallen' love** from the world [source above] of love, as mentioned by us numerous times; **and so how much more should I love the Creator blessed be He, that He is the Source of all the Pleasures.**

**Loose Translation:**

One of the mitzvos of the Torah is to love Hashem, but since Hashem Himself is Infinite and we are finite, His Essence will always remain unknown to us. The question then becomes how can we ever come to love Hashem if we do not know His Essence? The advice that the Torah gives us regarding how to do this, is through loving Hashem with *all* your heart, namely, even with the *yetzer* (pull) in your heart that is toward 'bad'. [The pull toward 'bad' (namely, extremes, see Rambam, *Shmoneh Prakim, Perek* 4) emanates from the part of the soul that is the *nefesh* (that relates to action) – the natural visceral animalistic pull in man – which naturally desires to enjoy the pleasures that are hidden within all the physical experiences of this world.]

The way to worship Hashem even through the physical pleasures of this world such as eating, drinking, etc. is to think to yourself [while you are partaking of that pleasure]: "Why do I love [the 'taste' of] this physical experience so much? It's because the pleasure that's in it is really connected to the Source of all pleasures above; if so, how much more should I love Hashem than I love the pleasurable experience that is within this physical object, because He is really the Infinite Source not only for *this* pleasure, but for all the pleasures that could possibly exist!!

התודה והברכה

לידידי היקר

ד"ר **אברהם היידימן** הי"ו

לעילוי נשמת אמו

**פראדל**

בת ר' מרדכי הלוי ע"ה


נ' ראש חודש שבט, תשע"ה לפ"ק

ת.נ.צ.ב.ה.


ויהי רצון שיזכה לראות נחת דקדושה
מכל יוצאי חלציו ולהתברך בהצלחה
ובסייעתא דשמיא בגשמיות וברוחניות

זו נדבת

ר״ר **פייבל יואל גלזר** הי״ו

לעילוי נשמת

אביו
# שרגא
בן אהרן ע״ה

נ׳ כ״ה ניסן, תשס״ט לפ״ק

אמו
# חיה רבקה
בת אברהם אבא ע״ה

נ׳ ה׳ מרחשון, תשס״ו לפ״ק

חמיו
# מיכאל
בן אשר ע״ה

נ׳ ו׳ מרחשון, תשנ״ח לפ״ק

חמותו
# שינה
בת דוב בער ע״ה

נ׳ י״ג כסלו, תשס״ט לפ״ק

ת.נ.צ.ב.ה.

זו נידב לכ' מחבר הספר

לכבוד ידידי

הרב **נחום** שליט"א

יעזור השם יתברך ויזכך להיות
ממזכי הרבים

ובפרט בספר זה שהיא הפצת ידיעות אמיתיות של
תורה בין כותלי בית המדרש

יברכך השם יתברך בהצלחה ובסייעתא דשמיא
בעבודתך עבודת הקודש לקרב ולחזק לבבות החלשות
ברוחניות ובגשמיות  כשאיפתך הטהורה
ואל תהא ברכת הדיוט קלה בעיניך

המברך בכל לב,

ידידך עוז,

הר"ר **יונה בלומנפרוכט** הי"ו

לכבוד ידידי היקר

ר"ר **דוד ווינבאך** הי"ו

יהי רצון שתזכה להצלחה
ולסייעתא דשמיא בגשמיות וברוחניות
ולכל טוב סלה

Special Thanks to
HIDABRUT
for their
support in this effort